THE PSYCHOLOGY OF WAR

THE PSYCHOLOGY OF WAR

COMPREHENDING ITS MYSTIQUE AND ITS MADNESS

Lawrence LeShan

The Noble Press, Inc.

CHICAGO

Printed in the United States of America

Library of Congress Cataloguing-in-Publication Data

LeShan, Lawrence
   The psychology of war: comprehending its mystique
   and its madness
   /   Lawrence LeShan.
               p.   cm.
         Includes bibliographical references.
         ISBN 1-879360-20-9   : $16.95
         1. War—Psychological aspects.   I. Title.
   U22.3.L45   1992
   355'.001'9—dc20   92-50438
                                           CIP

Noble Press books are available in bulk at discount prices.
Single copies are available prepaid direct from the publisher.

The Noble Press, Inc.
213 W. Institute Place, Suite 508
Chicago, Illinois 60610
(800) 486-7737

To
Earl Witenberg
Who helped me to a deeper understanding
of inner and outer wars

Let me have war, say I: It exceeds peace as far as day does night; it's spritely, waking, audible, full of vent. Peace is a very apoplexy, lethargy, mull'd, deaf, sleepy, insensible; a getter of more bastard children than war is a destroyer of men.

Shakespeare, *Coriolanus*, Act 4, Scene 5

No human inventory can fail to include our propensity for premeditated, organized murder of our fellows nor yet fail to notice that an army is a model of cooperation and self-sacrifice, or that no other species so carefully, tenderly cares for its wounded, even for its enemies.

Robert Ardrey, *The Hunting Hypothesis*

Men are interested in the outcomes of wars, not their causes.

Seneca

CONTENTS

Acknowledgements

This work would not have been possible without the generosity of the Fordham Library at Lincoln Center and its head, Clement J. Ansal, who gave me permission to use its excellent resources.

To Eda LeShan, whose contributions to this book are too many to list, my gratitude and love.

Introduction

"I would not," says Socrates, "be confident about everything I say about the argument: but one thing I would fight for to the end, both on word or deed if I were able—that if we believed we should try to find out what is not known, we should be better and braver and less idle than if we believed that what we do not know it is impossible to find out that we need not even try."

Plato, *The Meno*

THIS BOOK is an attempt to bring a new concept, recent to scientific thought, to bear on the problem of why human beings so universally and so frequently fight wars. We now understand that we habitually organize our perceptions of reality in a variety of ways, with the ability to shift from one way to another without necessarily being aware that we are doing so. None of these different ways of perceiving reality reveal the "truth" about the structure of the world and of ourselves any more than a cup, vase, or ashtray we fashion out of a lump of clay reveals the clay's "true" shape. Each has advantages and disadvantages, as does each of our differing ways of perceiving reality.

When we go to war, our perception of reality—of what we are and what is happening in the world around us—is quite different from that which we commonly use in peacetime. This shift, when it occurs, makes war much more difficult to prevent, or to stop once it has started. But understanding how and why this shift comes about allows us to see the signs that indicate a society is moving toward war, and to understand what has to be done to stop this movement.

The problem of why human beings go to war has been with us for a long time. Herodotus' great *The Histories*, written in the fifth century B.C., was primarily an attempt to understand the long enmity and conflict between the Greeks and Persians. Herodotus succeeded—to the degree that any of the countless

3

books on the causes of war have succeeded since then—in describing (correctly or incorrectly, according to changing views) the specific causes of one conflict. Other investigators have accomplished this purpose in looking at a great number of other conflicts, but attempts to generalize from their conclusions have not been successful. In the millennia between Herodotus and the present, a number of theories have been developed on why war is so widespread. None have been helpful in our attempts to put a stop to war.

Although each of these theories has proven itself convincing to different groups at different times, though never for longer than a brief period, none of them truly fits the overall data we have on how war happens. Lewis Fry Richardson's classic *The Statistics of Deadly Quarrels*, which presents an overview of the actual facts about when and under what conditions war occurs, has shown that none of our various accepted wisdoms on this subject have any validity. For example, people of my generation were brought up on the idea that the harsh peace treaties concluding World War I brought the next world war into being much more quickly. Richardson's analyses show the opposite—that statistically speaking, the harsher the peace treaty, the longer the period of peace that follows it. ("Statistical" relationships, of course, are different than "causal" relationships.) During the Crimean War, A. W. Kingslake put forth the theory that war is a foreign circus put on by rulers or ruling classes to distract citizens from troubles at home. As Richardson points out, this theory, attractive as it is in offering a simplified answer to the problem, does not fit the data at all. In World War I, for example, Germany's rulers were far more occupied with trying to unify the country in order to fight the war than with fighting the war in order to unify the country. Other widely believed theories have also fallen by the wayside, and no single theory is generally accepted today. There is wide disagreement among researchers in the social sciences on the subject of war and its causes; even within the individual disciplines, scholars who study war disagree with each other.

Further, as Geoffrey Blainey states in *The Causes of War*, his excellent and serious review of this field, it has become even more difficult to deal with the subject of war's causes today, when it has become ". . . almost a dogma that one nation or one group within each nation must be solely or mainly to blame for each war." Searching for someone or some group to blame, who is "the cause" for a problem, limits in advance the kind of solution to the problem we can perceive. This makes it far more difficult for us to see the larger question of why human beings follow a "culprit" into full-blown war.

War is not an entirely universal activity—there have always been a few cultures in which it is unknown or not understood. But under almost every condition of social, economic, and political organization, regardless of different family structures, child-rearing practices, and other social norms, people fight wars on a fairly regular basis.

There is today a great deal of discussion on the subject of using our present-day knowledge of psychology, sociology, and other social sciences to prevent war, and various action programs are attempting to put this knowledge to practical use. Common sense, as well as our scientific training, would seem to indicate that if we wish to limit a recurrent phenomenon, we need first to define the cause or causes of that phenomenon. It is no longer, for example, regarded as legitimate or intelligent medicine to try to cure a symptom without dealing with its cause. When this *is* done, the same or a related symptom generally breaks out again, sometimes in a worse form.

This brings us to the heart of the problem addressed in this book. A great deal has been done in the past, and is being done now, on *techniques*—such as intercultural student exchange, international organizations, international mediation efforts (i.e. the Camp David accords), and armament reduction—for reducing the likelihood of war. But very little has been done to address *why* human beings fight wars. There is, among social scientists interested in this problem, a readiness to deal with specific causes of specific wars. But there appears to be a great reluctance to deal with more general theories about the cause of war—or even to admit the necessity for such theories.

It is easy to start or join a crusade to prevent war: to encourage people of different nations to know each other better, to promote more enlightened child-rearing techniques, to stop hunger and economic deprivation, to increase education and literacy, and so forth. All of these are psychologically easy to appreciate and very much worth pursuing; whoever is not concerned with such issues has renounced his or her claim to membership in the human family. But for more effective progress we need a more scientific approach to the problem. Scientific method demands more than belief, passion, and dedication. It also demands active work in organizing knowledge, in order to think clearly about what we believe, what we know, and what we do not know. It is these qualities that are lacking in the work for peace.

* * *

In ancient times it was believed that there was only one cause of war, but there was disagreement as to what that particular cause was. Overall there were three basic theories advanced by thinkers in the classical world:

1) That war was inevitable given the nature of man; that all men had a basic instinct to acquire power, and this led inevitably to war.
2) That wars were fought for economic gain.
3) That man was a group animal, and that the nature and structure of groups led inevitably to war.

Whichever of these three basic theories a classical thinker espoused, he usually believed it explained *all* wars. Each of these theories remains alive in our modern era. Freud further developed the "psychological" theory that war is due to the basic nature of human beings; LeBon advocated the "social group" idea that war is due to the way humans function in groups; and Lenin and Rosa Luxemburg, among others, advanced the "economic," or "corn-and-iron" theory.

In 1910, Norman Angell wrote *The Great Illusion*, which was translated into eleven languages and discussed at all levels of influence in Europe. He characterized war as an economic activity, which had been valid in the past but was no longer feasible as the ratio of cost to profit in waging war had now reversed itself. Because of this, he said, there would be no more wars.

In 1911, General von Bernardi of the German General Staff published a widely read and influential book, *Germany and the Next War*. In it he described war as a "biological necessity."

Arthur Koestler, in his book *Janus*, brilliantly combined the "psychological" and "social group" theories of war and its causes. He saw humankind as having two basic drives: to individualize ourselves and to be part of a group. Most of us move erratically from one drive to the other. Koestler believed that men fight wars for reasons of group identification and loyalty—one widely used means of strengthening a group is to have an outside enemy.

Looking more closely at these theories—loosely categorizable into three "types"—we will see why they are not useful in terms of how we experience war today. Each has a grain of truth in it, and each has many devout believers who consider it the cause of *all* wars. In the end, however, none of them deal with the true scope of the problem, or can lead to useful solutions.

Throughout the history of man's ponderings over the problem of war, he has confused the stimuli—the specific events— which led to war with the problem of man's receptivity to these stimuli. For example, Herodotus reported the opinion that the long-term, destructive Greco-Persian conflict was caused by a series of kidnappings of women. I do not question here that specific events, or the drive for power of a leader, or a psychopath in a position of authority, may serve as the specific stimuli that set a war in motion. Rather I raise another, more basic question: why is man so willing to respond to these stimuli? If we can understand this, we can clarify some of the forces driving our repeated readiness to engage in armed, intergroup conflict.

Psychological Theories

Psychological theories concerning man's readiness to go to war are very old. In the classical world it was widely believed that all men desired power; that no matter how much power men had, they wanted more; and that this desire must inevitably lead to war. The surprise with which classical authors report exceptions to this (see, for example, Herodotus' discussion of Otanes, who did *not* want to be king of Persia) illustrates the strength of these beliefs. "Love of power," says Thucydides in *The Peloponnesian Wars*, "operating through greed and through personal ambition was the cause of all these evils." Other variations of the psychological theory have proposed that man is born evil, or that he is genetically an aggressive carnivore. Most psychological theories assume a basic conception of man akin to that of the philosopher Hobbes: there is something in man's nature that draws him to large-scale, overtly hostile action against his fellows.

On a much more complex and sophisticated level, Freud theorized that, because of an instinctual death drive that must be externalized if an individual is to avoid destroying himself, nothing can be done to stop war. The best we can do, said Freud, is await the time when mankind evolves further. In a famous exchange of letters, Einstein asked, "Why war?" and Freud answered, in effect, "Because man is what he is."

Obviously, if there is an inborn need in man to fight wars, then there is little that the scientist can hope to do about preventing them. He would be helpless against an organic part of man's nature. We may accept this theory as children of our culture; but do we also accept it in light of what we have learned from our present-day social sciences?

Instinct theories of human behavior are not in good repute today. We question the validity of an "instinct" for power, an instinct for aggression or murder. (Similarly, most social scientists question the existence of a "thanatos," a death instinct, as Freud envisioned it. Even in psychoanalytic circles, this concept has not gained wide acceptance.) Further, and more important, the *behavior* of our social scientists clearly indicates that we do not believe in psychological theories of war. An industrial psychologist acts to reduce hostility within a business organization. A social worker attempts to prevent hostile activity among juvenile gangs. A psychotherapist helps an aggressive patient find a way to live among other men without overt and violent conflict. *None of these professionals seem to believe that their work acts against the basic nature of man.* It therefore becomes clear that as scientists, we do not believe that man has something within him that must lead to warlike activity or to war itself. We act in ways clearly opposed to psychological theories of war. Simple and appealing as the concept is, we must reject the idea that it is inherent in man to fight wars—it is too clearly contradicted by the often successful work of our social scientists.

Economic Theories

The economic or "corn-and-iron" theories of the basic causes of wars are also very old. Livy wrote of Tarquin's preparing for war against Ardea, "Their wealth was, indeed, the reason for Tarquin's preparations. He needed money." Thucydides tells of the Corinthians urging their neighbors to join them as allies in a war to protect their import-export trade. According to the economic theory, man fights for wealth; he goes to war to obtain the goods and possessions of others.

It is obvious that since the Industrial Revolution, and beyond question since World War I, economic theories of war make no sense at all. The bald and unmistakably clear fact is that war destroys more capital and personal goods than the victor can possibly hope to take from the vanquished. To try to explain present international political tension on the ground that those involved believe war will increase their wealth is obvious nonsense.

In a nomad culture, or even in a pre-industrial culture, such economic theories may be valid. In a non-nomadic or a post-industrial culture, they are not. However, there have been no nomad cultures of importance for a long time, and post-industrial nations have frequently fought wars in this century.

Shall we go further and hypothesize that at one time wars *did* increase the wealth (or seemed to) of the victors, and that we continue to wage them either out of habit or as a sort of "phantom limb," a leftover behavior pattern from our past? The

9

"habit" hypothesis does not appear to be tenable. Our present knowledge of human behavior assures us that habits, per se, do not continue in the absence of any sort of motivation.

The "phantom limb" hypothesis is a more difficult one to understand. It assumes that men continue to believe something that was once true because they have not successfully reevaluated a particular situation. We know that this is not uncommon. However, *this* particular error—the mistaken idea that winning a war does bring profit—appears to have been clear to many leaders, both political and intellectual, at least since the last century. It has been repeatedly demonstrated to the world public. Where we might once have accepted economic gain as a possible motive behind war, we can no longer do so. In fact, the entire economic class of theory also must be rejected. When a man can produce so much more wealth as a worker than he can hope to gain as a soldier, it simply does not make sense to regard economic gain as a powerful force driving people toward war. Whatever its effect in the past, it is no longer a reasonable explanation. More importantly, we must ask: *even if there is a group of individuals who hope to profit from waging a war, why are they so enthusiastically followed by the rest of the citizens of their nation?*

Social Group Theories

This group of theories shares three basic tenets: first, that human beings exist in groups (as a result of their "nature," "economics," "early conditioning," or some other reason); second, that the behavior of groups is quite different from the behavior of individuals; and third, that inherent in the structure of human groups is overt intergroup hostility.

That human beings are group organisms, and that the behavior of groups may follow different laws than the behavior of individuals, are clearly true. However, the idea that groups are not only inevitably hostile to each other but also must express this hostility in open conflict is another matter. We all know of many established groups in close contact that do not seem to need to express hostility toward each other (e.g., the United

10

States and Canada). More to the point, however, we treat small and large groups quite differently. We do not act as if we regard intergroup conflict between small groups as inevitable. Rather we seem to believe that preventing overt conflicts and resolving covert conflicts are legitimate and reasonable goals of social science. Active group work, psychotherapy, city planning, and various techniques from industrial psychology are among the many tools we use, frequently with real success, in achieving these ends. It is only on the international level that we seem to regard conflict as inevitable and inexorable. Moreover, no one has organized any major research programs that might enable us to understand this problem better, and to ascertain whether we could control it through greater understanding.

It is startling to compare the time and energy expended by social scientists in the past fifty years in research on understanding and reducing aggression in juvenile gangs with the time and energy spent in research on understanding and reducing aggression between nations. Such a contrast, particularly at a point in time when the nations have atomic weapons and the juvenile gangs do not, is instructive. We are forced to conclude that an unverbalized assumption exists in these theories, that aggression is *not* organic to small groups, but *is* to large ones. This assumption does not appear to be a logical one. Therefore we cannot, as scientists, accept this group of theories as the answer to our question. It would involve us in too fundamental a paradox.

* * *

So far this discussion has been concerned with those theories of war that were first developed in the classical world. The reason for this is that these form the basis of our contemporary theories of war. Today our theories are more complex, and are based on more information than was available in the ancient world, but they still follow pretty much the same general lines.

The excellent review of this contemporary thought in the *Encyclopedia Britannica* (15th edition) states:

11

Contemporary theories of war divide roughly into two major schools. One attributes war to certain innate biological and psychological factors or drives, the other attributes it to certain social relations and institutions. Both schools include optimists and pessimists concerning the preventability of war.

The first group of theories—that there is something in the basic nature of human beings that leads them inevitably to war—falls, with a few exceptions, into two general classes. The first, mentioned earlier, are the Freudian theories that innate human destructive impulses must be turned either outward or inward. An inward turn destroys the individual; therefore, war is inevitable until we humans progress to a higher level of development.

The problem with this theory, as mentioned before, is that even those psychoanalysts who claim to accept it are working with patients to reduce outward expression of hostility, without believing that they are thereby forcing the patient to turn his destructive impulses against himself. As a theory Freud's is of interest, at least historically. In actuality, it has not proven to be of any use in either work with individuals or work with international conflict. Freud himself later said that he found his answer to Einstein's question as to "Why war?" ("Because man is what he is") to be sterile and unsatisfactory.

Another prevalent psychoanalytic theory holds that the individual displaces his own childhood hostilities and aggressions to whatever enemy his society provides. Karl Menninger put it:

> War is a reflection of multiple . . . miniature wars in the hearts of individuals. . . . The war of nations is a magnification of the war of human instincts, human motives. . . . It is absurd to deny that there are social pressures, but social pressures result from the accumulation and organization of the child's individual experience with his parents.

Certainly there is some truth in this concept. The "steam" behind our joining together to go to war against a culturally defined enemy must have some source. We get excited and stimulated when our group is deciding to take an active part in any hostilities. With a clean conscience, we follow the ancient tradition of loading our sins, our guilt, and our hatreds onto one object, and then attacking that object. These theories are founded on the idea that individual hostility is displaced to a foreign state instead of being focused on another person. The basic concept is that of the hydraulic pump; hostility is conceptualized as a fluid under pressure which can be squirted out either one nozzle or another.

As a full explanation for war's existence, however, this does not really work. War is, for a great many, a dispassionate activity; for some it is even an opportunity to engage in particular kinds of intellectual activity. By and large, those who plan the actual killing are far removed from it. It is doubtful that an Eisenhower, a Patton, a Rommel, a Grant, or a Lee ever personally killed anyone else once they reached their elevated rank.

Further, different kinds of child-rearing procedures among different cultures do not seem to create major differences in tendencies toward war. Many of the American Plains Indian tribes were very loving toward children and regarded anyone who struck a child as insane. (Some of the tribes, it is said, knew that peace with the white man was impossible, because white people were all crazy—they actually *hit* their children!) However, these same tribes were very frequently at war with each other. Finally, not even the psychoanalytic societies (made up of well-analyzed members who presumably have explored and are at ease dealing with their own hostilities) are known for their pacifist tendencies. No one has seen them take a visible stand against war.

The other primary class of contemporary theories in this group stems out of hypotheses about human history and racial development. Robert Ardrey, among others, believes that for a very long time the human race were hunters, and that this behavior has become part of our genetic heritage. According to Ardrey, war is an outgrowth of hunting, and armies and the "military virtues" are offshoots of the hunting party and its necessary codes of behavior.

This theory basically holds that the human brain has a history, and that this history is shaped by the millions of years in which humans were hunters. Ardrey estimates that we hunted for between 500,000 and 2,500,000 years, and that we have raised crops and domestic animals for only about 5,000 years: "For a mere one percent of the history of true man, we have lived under conditions which we regard as normal." This, he says, accounts for our fascination with the chase and kill (see the majority of successful television series), with weapons, and with the self-sacrifice of the individual to the group. What we call military virtues are the same as those of the successful hunting group made up of individuals too weak to hunt alone: courage, cooperation, personal responsibility, loyalty, self-sacrifice, concerted action, leadership. Man, according to this viewpoint, loves war because he is essentially a hunter, and because his evolution was marked irrevocably by his history of hunting.

The logical extension of this idea would be that war should appear in human history only after we turned to a non-hunting life, when idled hunters acted out their historical imperative by hunting each other in large groups. However, the agricultural revolution was only just beginning to get under way in 6,500 B.C., and the walls of Jericho, which date from this era, could only have been built by a people accustomed to war, with the long experience and cultural development necessary to create such sophisticated defense systems.

Konrad Lorenz has developed a similar theory, but one that goes back even further in human history and development. Animals that can kill each other easily, he theorizes, have developed inhibition mechanisms that largely prevent them from killing their own kind. A raven, with its killer bill, is inhibited from killing other ravens; similarly, the lion and the wolf generally do not kill their own. Animals that cannot easily kill each other—such as the dove, the ape, and man—have had no need to develop such inhibitory instincts. Humans, however, developed the techniques to kill each other with one blow (or, even more recently, one crook of the index finger), without developing the inhibitions that would prevent their use. Therefore we murder each other and go to war.

This theory rests in part on the idea that war exists at the far end of a scale of hostile activity, at the other end of which is personal violence against another individual—murder. There is, however, no reason to suppose this idea true, attractive and simple as it seems. Koestler, in *Janus* and elsewhere, has shown that the fighting humans participate in during a war is done primarily for reasons of group loyalty and idealism. Where murder is usually committed for self-assertive reasons, Koestler has shown—and modern studies of soldiers at war strongly bear this out—that war is fought primarily for self-transcending reasons. It is, says Koestler:

> ... one of the ironies of the human condition that its ferocious destructiveness derives not from the self-assertive, but from the integrative potential of the species.

Most anthropologists strongly disagree with the instinctual and developmental argument for war's existence. Ashley Montagu observed:

> The development of intelligence increasingly freed man from the bondage of biologically predetermined response mechanisms .... far from being innate, human aggressiveness is a learned form of behavior.

In 1967 a special plenary session of the American Anthropological Association on war and its causes concluded that instinct theories are simply not in accordance with the evidence; that the location of war's origins in animal ethnology are not useful; and that in this sense, at least, human beings are qualitatively different from animals. The overall response of the anthropologists to the instinct theories of war was probably best given by Ruth Benedict:

> There are societies where Nature perpetuates the slightest mode of behavior by biological mechanisms, but these are societies not of men but of the social insects. ... For better or for worse man's solution lies at the opposite pole. Not one item of his tribal social organization, of his language, of his local religion, is carried in his germ cells. ... Culture is not a biologically transmitted complex.

The disparity between animals and man in this regard is also shown in Samuel Johnson's well-known fable of the two vul-

15

tures talking about the strange phenomenon of humans killing each other in large numbers from time to time and then leaving the corpses without eating them. To kill not for food is so strange and beyond their experience that they cannot find a reason for it. One of them has heard of a very old, very wise vulture who pondered this problem all his life. He finally came to the conclusion that humans are not animals at all, but vegetables with the power of motion, and that just as the wind shakes oak trees, some unaccountable wind shakes humanity from time to time. When this happens, men kill each other as meaninglessly as acorns fall from the trees. The idea of war as a factor differentiating animals from humans has been known and discussed since Roman times.

On leaving this very quick overview of instinctivist theories of war, it makes sense to look briefly at the idea that war is good for people. Over and over, poets, philosophers, and historians have written that peace brings decay and the withering of worthwhile virtues, what Kipling called "honor and faith and a sure intent." Whether offered by the Roman poet Juvenal:

> Now we suffer the evils of long peace. Luxury hatches terrors worse than wars.

the philosopher Hegel:

> War has the higher meaning that through it . . . the ethical health of nations is maintained.

the physical anthropologist Sir Arthur Keith:

> Nature keeps her orchard healthy by pruning; war is her pruning hook.

a member of the German General Staff during World War I:

> Perpetual peace is a dream and not even a beautiful dream, and War is an integral part of God's ordering of the universe. In War, man's noblest virtues come into play: courage and renunciation, fidelity to duty and a readiness for sacrifice that does not stop short of offering up Life itself. Without War the world would become swamped in materialism.
> Hellmuth von Moltke

or even Mussolini himself

> War alone brings all human energies to their highest tension and sets a seal of nobility on peoples who have the virtue to face it.
>
> *The Doctrine of Fascism*

these sentiments appear across cultures and through the ages. Whatever their validity in the past (and I see none), they have certainly been invalid since August 6, 1945, when the sorrow and shame of Hiroshima ushered us from one period of history into the next. With any future wars meaning the possible destruction of our species, it is clear that whether or not war had any virtues in the past, it certainly does not in the present. A cartoon in the March 25, 1991, issue of *The New Yorker* shows two cavemen talking. One of them is saying: "I'd be the first to say 'Repeal the harsh old rule of tooth and claw' if somebody could show me that it wasn't working." The thousands and thousands of atomic weapons in the world's armories, and the certainty that someone is going to use them if we continue our present patterns of international relations, are evidence that it isn't working.

The second principal group of modern theories on war, as defined by the *Britannica*, focuses primarily on social institutions; and has been carried furthest by socialist theoreticians. In large part these thinkers followed the lead of nineteenth-century sociologists such as Saint-Simon and Spencer, who adhered to a dual conception of social structures that contrasted societies based on peaceful labor and exchange with societies dominated by a military caste and motivated by ambition for war and conquest. This dualism was widely accepted in the nineteenth century, though it is no longer adhered to by most sociologists.

The socialist viewpoint holds that war is an inevitable aspect of the class struggle. When the proletariat has finally triumphed (as it must, of historical necessity), then and only then will war be abolished. In Lenin's words:

> We socialists understand that war cannot be abolished *unless classes are abolished and socialism is created* [Lenin's italics]; and we also differ (from the bourgeois, pacifists, and the anar-

chists) in that we regard civil war, i.e., wars waged by the oppressed class, slaves against slave owners, by serfs against landowners, and wage earners against the bourgeoisie, as fully legitimate, progressive and necessary.

Lenin and other socialist theoreticians of his time distinguish three classes of conflict into which all wars fit: those between capitalist states for raw materials, markets, and so on; those between capitalist and socialist states expressing the class struggle; and colonial wars of liberation.

The socialist conception of war was further developed chiefly by Rosa Luxemburg. As she saw it, wars were essentially a result of the pressures of international market economics:

> Capitalist economy cannot, because of its very structure, absorb its own production and is therefore compelled to expand: the individual is not even aware of the mechanism that is carrying him away.

Although the theories of Lenin and Luxemburg have enjoyed much prestige and acceptance, they simply do not fit the actual data. Many wars fought during this century (e.g. World War II) bear no relation at all to Lenin's definitions. As to the views of Rosa Luxemburg, the twenty years preceding World War I were in fact among the most prosperous in the history of capitalism— or indeed of known history. Markets for manufactured goods abounded and new ones were constantly appearing. The standard of living, prices, mechanization, technological know-how —all were steadily increasing. A very good case could be made that overall, the economic burden of World Wars I and II fell more heavily on the owners of capital than on wage earners. Economic considerations forcing Europe to destroy itself seems a dubious conclusion, to say the least.

A detailed analysis by K. F. Otterbain shows that economic factors appear to have little influence on the outbreak of war. And contrary to the socialist view, war is perfectly possible between socialist states. It was only because the USSR was so overwhelmingly powerful that war was avoided between it and Hungary and Czechoslovakia in 1951. The world also trembled on the brink of war between China and the USSR several times.

By and large, Marxist theorists are not much interested in the question studied in this book. From their viewpoint, people go to war because of their class identification and are on one side or the other of the struggle between proletariat and bourgeoisie. However, in every war over the past century or so, workers, factory owners, farmers, capitalists, and bourgeoisie all appeared equally enthusiastic and ready for battle to commence.

* * *

This book brings not only the thought of the past 2,500 years to bear on the problem of war, but also a new conceptual tool, one that has previously been unavailable to us. For the past thirty years, I have been involved in a new field of thought that analyzes the different ways human beings conceptualize reality—how we determine who we are, and the nature of the cosmos in which we live—and the effects of these different conceptions on our feelings and behavior.

This field first gained legitimacy and coherence when Max Planck invented quantum theory early in this century. He pointed out that we do not live in a one-track universe, but a multi-track one. This marked the beginning of science's turn from attempting to discover the "truth" of reality, to attempting to discover more fruitful ways to organize reality, to construe it. The new view held that any such "truth" was not ultimately discoverable and that there was no "right" way to organize our impressions about the world, but rather a number of more or less useful ways for solving different specific problems.

In spite of the tremendous development of this new view provided by William James in *The Pluralistic Universe*, in 1909, and later by the work of Ernst Cassirer, it has only been in the past quarter-century that we have begun to understand its implications for human thought, feeling, and behavior. It is the application of this new understanding to our conception of war and its causes that is the special contribution of this book.

ONE

The Human Attraction to War

The fact is, unfortunately, that hatred in the public sense makes people's eyes bright, starts the adrenalin flowing, as love in the public sense does not. People feel fine when they are full of anger and hatred against someone else.

May Sarton, *At Seventy*

IT IS CLEAR from all of human history that our drive to armed, intergroup conflict is extremely strong. Nothing human beings have ever done has been able to end war for very long. In the medieval era, for example, when the power of organized religion was at its height, the Catholic church made massive efforts to restrict warfare to certain days of the week and to prohibit the crossbow as "inhumane." The church was completely unsuccessful in both endeavors. Not only has organized religion been unable to *prevent* war, it has been unable to control it or to prevent any sort of military action once a war has started. In the words of a medieval manuscript, the *Zohar*, "When men are at war, even God's anger does not frighten them."

Not only has organized religion been helpless in the face of war, so also has been our intellectual culture. With the exception of Bertrand Russell, no first-rate philosopher in our history has consistently advocated peace. In all the major wars of this century, the educated classes voted for war policies and enlisted in the army as readily and enthusiastically as did their less educated compatriots.

The men who planned bureaucratic homicide in Vietnam were among our best: They were Rhodes Scholars, university professors, business leaders, war heroes. All men who had succeeded brilliantly in their careers. They were models of respectability and achievement. They were superior by almost any accepted definition of the society.

Richard J. Barnet, *The Roots of War*

Though this century has seen the world reach the highest level of per capita education in human history, it has also, as the sociologist Pitirim Sorokim has pointed out, been one of the bloodiest in history.

Nor have social orientation and commitment to pacifism been a useful counterforce to the movement toward war. Although in the eighteenth and nineteenth centuries (from Thomas Paine onward) it was an article of faith among liberals that universal suffrage would end war, "because the people would certainly vote out of office any belligerently inclined government," the twentieth century has shown clearly that this is not so. In 1913, for example, the International Socialist movement was very strong in Europe and was completely opposed to war. By 1914 every Socialist party in Europe had reversed its stand and was strongly in support of its country's participation in the new war. On July 31, 1914 (the day before Germany declared war on Russia), Jean Jaures, head of the strongly internationalist French Socialist party, wrote in *L'Humanite*: "Man has an irremediable need to save his family and country even through armed nationalism." Other social philosophies have fared no better in effecting a consistent and effective opposition to war.

Given the data we have on the almost universal occurrence, frequency, and popularity of war, it is clear that war *promises* something to human beings, promises to fulfill some need or combination of needs that are at least close to universal. Whatever the tension is that war promises to ease, it seems to be present in nearly all cultures and in all of the different socioeconomic, political, and intellectual strata of these cultures. We are dealing here with what is clearly a fundamental human tension.

Further, it is a *specifically* human tension. The only animals that wage war are human beings and harvester ants. The ants do it for strictly economic reasons—to increase their food supply.

As I have indicated, such an economic justification simply does not explain war among humans. In any case, since we have learned nothing useful about the psychology of human beings from studying white rats, greylag geese, or pigeons, it is highly unlikely that we can learn much about our propensity for war from the study of one specific breed of ants.

* * *

There is one "basic," or at least almost universal, tension that seems restricted to human beings. This is the problem of how to be both an individual and a part of something larger than oneself. A cat appears to have no trouble being a cat, experiencing both its own uniqueness and its relationships among other cats. To a cat these two needs seem to offer no contradictions; to a human being they very often do. A dog apparently has no trouble being Rover, a beagle, and a dog, all at the same time. A human being frequently has a great deal of trouble being John, a salesman, a husband, an American, and a human being.

If we look through present-day academic textbooks in subjects such as psychology, sociology, and anthropology, we see instance after instance of the constant conflict and interplay between these two forces. On the one hand is the drive to be more and more *oneself*, more and more unique and individual, to heighten and strengthen one's experience and being. On the other hand is the drive to be accepted as a member of a group, not to stand apart as an outsider, in order to be a full-fledged member of the tribe.

All through our development we have to deal with the tension between these two drives. The infant slowly separates himself from others. The adolescent has a fierce desire to be accepted by the group, picking his clothes and altering his behavior in terms of group dictates. The adult struggles with the problem of how much he can behave in individual ways and how much he needs to conform to group standards.

Whatever we call this tension—whether a conflict between ego needs and affiliative needs; between socialization and individuation; between ego instincts and libidinal instincts; between a need to belong and a need to individualize and articulate oneself; or between shame and ontological guilt—the terminology is not critical here. This tension is strong enough and widespread enough that a wide variety of such terms is needed to think clearly about it.

Many of the great works in our literature reflect this theme, dealing over and over with the problem of how to reconcile the conflict between these two drives. There are the tragedies of Willy Loman and George F. Babbitt, who gave up their individuality for roles and behaviors that they believed would lead them to be accepted and respected by others, and were thereby destroyed. Among those who went to the opposite extreme and were also thereby destroyed, Macbeth and Richard III come quickly to mind. Prince Myshkin in Dostoevesky's *The Idiot* deals with this tension in one way: Dr. Stockmann in Ibsen's *An Enemy of the People* in another.

One aspect of this tension is revealed in Schopenhauer's charming discussion of how a man and a woman relate to each other, which he illustrates using the story of the cold porcupines. One winter in a cave, runs the story, there were two porcupines. Feeling both the cold of the winter and the existential cold of the universe, they huddled together for mutual warmth. However, when their spines stuck into one another's skin, they had to draw apart. Slowly they moved together and apart, trying to solve this complicated problem, which was made worse by the fact that one had longer spines than the other and that the tenderness of their skins also differed. Finally they found the ideal distance where each received the maximum warmth from the other and neither's spines penetrated the other's skin.

As crucial as our individual uniqueness is to us, we all know we must identify ourselves with something larger than our skin-limited being; alone, we lose something of our humanness. Even the hermit is connected with others through a vision, whether it be of God, Brahma, or some other universal. (Indeed, Thomas Merton has pointed out that the hermit retires *to* the world, not from it.) As the philosopher Hannah Arendt put it:

No human life, not even the life of the hermit in nature's wilderness, is possible without a world which directly or indirectly testifies to the presence of other human beings.

If a primate expert such as Wolfgang Kohler could say "A solitary chimpanzee is not a chimpanzee," what could we say of a truly solitary human being? For those who do not identify themselves with at least one larger group of other humans, we have only pity or contempt. In Sir Walter Scott's words:

> This wretch concentered all in self
> Living shall forfeit all renown
> And doubly dying shall go down
> To that vile dust from which he sprung
> Unwept, unhonored and unsung.

"Life," wrote Hegel, "to be of value must hold an object of value in front of it." This object involves relationships with other human beings. In biological terms, we would have a hard time surviving alone. As Naomi Remen has shown, premature infants who are frequently touched and held have a far higher survival rate than their untouched and unheld peers. Children born at nine months will simply waste away if not given affection and physical contact. As adults, if we withdraw too much and have too little identification and contact with others, or with the larger issues of humanity, we may not immediately notice the damage it does to us, but that damage will show up in time. In an Eastern "wisdom" story, a Sufi (holy man) says to his disciples, "See that woodchopper with the fresh cut branch over his shoulder. The leaves are alive and juicy. They do not know that they have been cut off from their source. But they will learn. They will learn."

We know today that these two conflicting drives, the need to be an individual and the need to be part of a larger whole, though apparently so antithetical in nature, in actuality depend on each other. A "healthy" (i.e., self-satisfying, permitting of further growth, contributing to self-esteem) development of one drive relies on the development of the other. "It is," wrote the mystic Evelyn Underhill, "a paradox of our amphibious condition that we can only develop so far in one without a corresponding development of the other." The psychologist Erik Erikson much preferred to term our being a "psychosocial identity" rather than an "ego identity." He believed that the social aspects of our individual lives are at least as important as the ego aspects.

This knowledge is, of course, far from new. In the words of St. Thomas Aquinas, *"Homo est naturaliter politicus, id est socialis."* (Man is by nature political, that is, social.)

Koestler has described human beings as "holons": literally, he says, we are like the Roman god Janus, a being with two faces looking in opposite directions. He describes the reconciliation of this duality as the greatest struggle of our lives, and our whole development a back-and-forthing in our definitions of ourselves. Both sides are necessary: take away one and the other ceases to exist. Stabilization is exceedingly difficult; we always want more of both halves, and yet believe that each can only be bought at the expense of the other.

* * *

Historically and anthropologically, there are two different means (both of which appear in nearly every known human culture) available to us that promise to satisfy both of these drives, simultaneously and without contradiction.

A very small part of the human race turns to one of the schools of esoteric or spiritual development. Throughout history and our present age, some version of these appears in every society of which we have records. They are generally, although not always, allied with religious groups, and come under such names as Zen; Christian, Hindu, or Jewish mysticism; or Sufism.

All of these different schools agree that there are two ways of "being-in-the-world," of construing the self and the universe. In one of these (generally called "The Way of the Many"), we are each separate and individual, moving through the world one by one and communicating with each other through sound and signal. In the other ("The Way of the One"), we are all a part of the total cosmos; nothing within it, including ourselves, is separate from anything else. We communicate with each other as part of the same "seamless garment" that includes all reality. In the first way we exist as separate notes: in the second we exist as part of the symphony of all being. The metaphor of seeing a painting as individual brush strokes or as an integrated whole also applies to this duality.

All different schools of mystic thought agree that humans have what the Roman mystic Plotinus called an "amphibious nature," and need to develop and integrate both ways of being, The Way of the One and The Way of the Many, in order to survive, let alone reach our full potential as human beings. All offer techniques to enhance both modes of being in ways that don't create contradiction. On the one hand, the lengthy, difficult techniques of meditation these schools espouse all increase sharpness of perception, heighten a sense of self, and increase a sense of *individual* being. On the other hand, these same techniques will also lead to a more profound sense of *oneness* with all existence. The schools insist there is no contradiction here.

Although these schools have been widespread in different historical eras and cultures, they all require an intensive discipline that only a small part of the human race has ever been able to achieve. In spite of the very high caliber of many of their members, their overall influence has been small. Although they promise—and apparently often deliver—a solution to a deep and basic human tension, the path they offer is too long and difficult for most of us.

* * *

Historically there is a second means of resolving this tension between our need for singularity and our need for group identification. This means also appears in nearly every culture, and it too promises to fulfill *both* of these needs simultaneously, without contradiction; it promises to enhance our individuality and heighten our existence and, at the same time, increase our sense of being part of a group; to lessen our separateness at the same time it increases our individuality. Further, it promises to do so with full social approval and without the arduous discipline required for meditation, which apparently can only be followed by a few.

This second path is the way of armed group conflict—of war. Tolstoy described its effect in *War and Peace*:

> Every general and every soldier was conscious of his own significance, feeling himself but a grain of sand in the ocean of humanity, and at the same time was conscious of his might, feeling himself a part of the whole.

Again and again, descriptions of war both by experienced participants and by great artists (and Tolstoy was both) demonstrate that it fulfills both of these fundamental needs, simultaneously and without contradiction. It sharpens experience, increases the height and brilliance of perception, and makes one more and more aware of one's own existence. At the same time, war offers us the opportunity to become part of something larger and more intense—to be a note that has blended into a symphony. The Way of the One and the Way of the Many are followed simultaneously, and each intensifies the other.

William Manchester writes of his intense training in Marine boot camp at Parris Island in World War II:

> Everything I saw seemed so exquisitely defined—every leaf, every pebble looked as sharp as a drawing in a book. I knew I was merely a tiny cog in the vast machine which would confront fascism, but that was precisely why I had volunteered.

Out of his long experience as an infantryman in World War I, Erich Maria Remarque created *All Quiet on the Western Front*, where he wrote:

> We feel that in our blood a contact had shot home. This is no figure of speech, it is a fact. It is the front, the consciousness of the front that makes this contact . . . there is suddenly in our veins, in our hands, in our eyes, a tense waiting, a profound growth, a strange sharpening of the senses. The body with one bound is in full readiness. . . . Perhaps it is our inner and most secret life that falls on guard.

> We sit opposite one another. . . . We don't talk much but I believe we have a more complete communion with one another than ever lovers have. We are two men, two minute sparks

of life; outside is the night and the circle of death. . . . We sit . . . and feel in unison and are so intimate that we do not even speak.

I am no longer a shredding spark of existence, alone in the darkness; I belong to them and they to me, we all share the same life, we are nearer than lovers, in a simple, a harder way.

The writer Jo Coudert recounts:

And in England, shortly after the war, I commented to a Londoner what a relief it must have been to have the bombings ended. "Oh" she said, "it was a marvelous time. You forgot about yourself and you did what you could and we were all in it together. It was frightening, of course, and you worried about getting killed, but in some ways it was better than now. Now we're all just ourselves again."

These quotations are not from individuals who glorify war in any way. Their comments come from their experience of both what war promises and what it delivers. It is crucial to understand why war is so popular among humankind; if we understand the dynamic of its popularity, we can see begin to find new ways to act against its recurrence.

* * *

Certainly what war promises differs from what it delivers. Nevertheless it does deliver temporary solutions to psychological problems for a very large percentage of the population. And once a war begins the social pressures to continue it are very strong. Anyone who raises questions about a war while it is going on is considered a traitor or a lapsed heretic, and such people traditionally are imprisoned or killed. One cannot question the accepted wisdom that the war being waged is a wonderful crusade to rid the world of evil.

During World War I many people living in Allied nations knew of the Briey Salient, where 40 percent of Germany's steel was manufactured within easy sight and range of Allied artillery; but the steel factories there (which were owned by international cartels) were never shelled. Many knew that Germany's excellent Fokker fighter planes were made with

French aluminum, which was exported daily through Switzerland and sold to Germany. During the first part of World War II, this pattern continued. After the declaration of war and up to the Blitzkrieg, a half-million tons of French steel were sold to Germany, via Belgium, each month. During a war, no one prints such facts or talks about them very much.

After a war is over, with the general disillusionment and social discoherence that accompanies the failure of the post-war dream, no one cares to examine these sorts of contradictions. It is all better forgotten, and when Johnny comes marching home with a chronic disability from his wounds, we all try to forget our recent bout of psychological illusion. We try to put the mess out of our minds as soon as possible.

* * *

There are three ideas that, when they appear in society, should be regarded as signals that we are moving toward war, and that it is time to take strong action against this drift:

1. The idea that there is a particular enemy nation that embodies evil, *and that if it were defeated, the world would become paradise.* (It is the latter part of this statement that is crucial as a danger signal. The first part may well be true—as with Tamerlane's hordes or Hitler's Germany.)
2. The idea that taking action against this enemy (now *the* enemy) is the path to glory and to legendary heights of existence.
3. The idea that anyone who does not agree with this accepted wisdom is a traitor.

These three danger signals frequently appear reciprocally between two enemy nations, which probably increases the speed of their progression into armed conflict. If they appear in only one, and that nation then attacks its enemy, then the enemy nation is likely to believe that it has been attacked without warning (the great majority of wars start with an armed attack preceding a declaration of war); this in turn increases that nation's sense that its attacker is evil.

The way that people perceive reality in the period typically preceding the outbreak of war is very attractive in itself, as we will see. I will call this sort of perception the "mythic" mode, as opposed to the "sensory" mode of perception we ordinarily use. As we shift to the mythic mode in a pre-war period, we are also—without knowing it—making it much more likely that war will break out.

Robert E. Lee was wrong when he said, "It is well that war is so terrible—we would grow too fond of it." We are already far too fond of it, as any history book will show. It is only when we accept this that we will be able to deal with war's basic cause— the human attraction to war—and hope to end war altogether.

TWO

War and the Perception of Reality

When the banner is unfurled, all reason is in the trumpet.

> Ukrainian proverb

A rational army would run away.

> Montesquieu

Man aggresses not only out of frustration and fear but out of joy, plentitude, love of life. Men kill lavishly out of the sublime joy of heroic triumph over evil. . . . Most men will not usually kill unless it is under the banner of some kind of fight against evil. . . . I think it is time for social scientists to catch up with Hitler as a psychologist, and to realize that men will do anything for heroic belonging to a victorious cause if they are persuaded about the legitimacy of that cause.

> Ernest Becker, *Escape from Evil*

Our world has sprouted a weird concept of security and a warped sense of morality. Weapons are sheltered like treasures and children are exposed to incineration.

> Bertrand Russell

THE MOST IMPORTANT QUESTION to ask when considering war is why wars are so frequent *now*—well after the Industrial Revolution. We know conclusively that war destroys far more wealth than it produces; that it is usually fought (for most of the developed countries involved) so far from home that explanations such as "territoriality" are clear nonsense; and that it is fought so dispassionately by planners and administrators, and at such long range (even by many actual combatants such as artillerymen, bomber crews, and rocket units) that "displaced aggression" and "pugnacious instinct" theories are simply and clearly not relevant.

In spite of these facts, war is still extremely popular among human beings. The dozens of wars waged around the world throughout the course of this century illustrate this. We may or may not be dealing with the same dynamic sequences leading to war that were at work in 450 B.C., 1200 A.D., and the 1600s. In any case, we must—for practical reasons, remaining ever mindful of the lessons of the past—look to the present. The world changed for all of us and changed forever on August 6, 1945, when a bit of the sun was ignited over Hiroshima. However, we can look at the process of moving from peace to war as requiring the same dynamic motivating forces throughout the last century and a half. These are *our* times, and it is in them that we must solve this problem. "History took my generation by the throat in 1914," wrote Arnold Toynbee, and neither his nor succeeding generations have ever recovered.

* * *

It is important to note at this point that a "nation" does not exist except in the minds, and on the maps, of human beings— those of its own citizens and those of the citizens of other "nations." To say "A nation responds . . . " or "France struck back at the invader" makes for good poetry, but is semantic nonsense. Human beings, usually living in a specific geographical area, and regarding themselves as citizens of a political entity, may act together in a military manner; but there is no meaning in saying that a "nation" takes military action. People often (perhaps typically) act as if their nation is a biological organism, with a will of its own, but it is individuals who act, not nations. Not being clear on this point (and most writers on war have not been) is bound to lead to confusion.

* * *

To begin an analysis of the processes leading to war, let us look at the different ways in which reality is viewed in peacetime and in wartime. To examine these differences as clearly as possible, we will compare the perceived situation at the beginning of a crisis that terminated in armed conflict with the perceived situation after war has been declared and fighting actually started.

When we examine how we perceive and experience reality—"what is"—in peacetime and in wartime, we are startled at the difference between these two perceptions. What follows are a few illustrations of this difference.

PEACETIME	WARTIME
1. Good and Evil have many shades of gray. Many groups with different ideas and opinions are legitimate. Their opinions, and things in general, are relatively good or bad, satisfactory or unsatisfactory, stupid or intelligent.	Good and Evil are reduced to Us and Them. There are no innocent bystanders; there are only those for or those against us. The crucial issues of the world are divided into black and white. Opinions on these matters are absolutely right or absolutely wrong.
2. Now is pretty much like other times. There are more of some things, less of others, but the differences are quantitative.	Now is special, qualitatively different from all other times. Everything is cast in the balance; whoever wins now wins forever. It is the time of the final battle between good and evil—of Armageddon, of Ragnarok, of The War to End All Wars.
3. The great forces of nature, such as God or human evolution, are not particularly involved in our disputes.	"Gott Mit Uns," "Manifest Destiny," "Dieu et mon Droit," "History fights on our side," and other such slogans indicate our belief that the great motivating forces of the cosmos are for Us
4. When this present period is over, things will go on pretty much as they have in the past.	When this war is over, everything will be vastly different. If we win, it will be much better; if we lose, terribly worse. The world will be deeply changed by what we do here. Winning or losing will change the meaning of the past and the shape of the future.

5. There are many problems to be solved and their relative importance varies from day to day. Life is essentially complex, with many foci.	There is only one major problem to be solved. All others are secondary. Life is essentially simple. It has one major focus.
6. All people act from pretty much the same motives.	They act from a wish for power. We act from self-defense, benevolence, and reasons of common decency and morality.
7. Problems start on many different levels, whether economic, political, or personal, and must be dealt with on these levels.	The real problem started with an act of will on the part of the enemy and can only be solved by breaking his will or by making him helpless to act on it.
8. We are concerned with the causes of the problems we are trying to solve.	We are not concerned with causes, only with outcomes.
9. We can talk with those we disagree with. Negotiation is possible.	Since the enemy is evil, he naturally lies. Communication is not possible. Only force can settle the issue. *We* tell the truth (news, education). *They* lie (propaganda).
10. All people are fundamentally the same. Differences are quantitative.	"We" and "They" are qualitatively different, so different that the same actions are "good" when we do them, and "evil" when the enemy does them. There is doubt that we and they really belong to the same species.

What is outlined here clearly involves a shift in the perception of reality, an essential change from our structuring the world in our customary way to our structuring it in the ways of a fairy tale or a myth. The way-things-are, the rules for living, the morality that guides us: all of these qualities are very different during peacetime than in wartime.

The difference is even greater than one would assume from the bare descriptions listed above. Sweet and adorable Dorothy, whom all of us love and whom none of us would condemn, travels from everyday, common-sense-reality Kansas to mythic-reality Oz. While there she kills two people, the Wicked Witches of the North and of the South. Since they are not only bad, but exist in a mythic structure of reality where "bad" means "ultimately and completely evil," we applaud. But there is also a bad woman in Kansas, Miss Gulch, who tries to have Toto killed and bedevils Dorothy quite severely. What would have happened to our feelings for Dorothy if she had killed that woman in Kansas —even accidentally? At the very least, most of us would have wavered in our unqualified approval.

The situation is similar during wartime. The enemy is so completely, so *mythically* evil that almost anything we do to him is not only justified, but good. As Rollo May puts it:

> At the outset of every war . . . we hastily transform our enemy into the image of the daimonic; and then, since it is the devil we are fighting, we can shift onto a war footing without asking ourselves all the troublesome and spiritual questions that the war arouses. We no longer have to face the realization that those we are killing are persons like ourselves.

This statement is true, but leaves out an essential fact. The "daimonic" can only fit into a "mythic reality"; we have little room or patience for this concept in our everyday "sensory reality," the reality in which we (in peacetime) live most of our lives. If our car breaks down on a stormy night in the country, we might think it was caused by bad luck or evil forces, but we know the real solution to this problem lies in finding a good repairman, with his common sense, experience, and technical skills. And after the car is repaired, no matter what our hurry, we would not run over a child to complete our journey. This is the nature of sensory reality. However, the training in high-tech mass destruction we give to bomber pilots is simply a tool used in a "great cause." We would, with no particular compunctions, bomb a city filled with ten thousand sleeping children in the mythic reality of wartime.

If we wish to understand what is going on here, we must look not only at the killing and willingness to kill characteristic of people during wartime, but also at how these are an integral part of a particular "reality," and how that reality works. These two realities—mythic and sensory—are structurally different, and this difference leads inexorably to differences in thought and behavior. In the mythic reality that characterizes a society at war, these differences result in a world where everything is black or white and there are no shades of gray.

No important characters in *Cinderella* are half good and half bad. The stepmother and stepsisters are all bad. Nothing they think or do is good. Cinderella herself, the Fairy Godmother, and the Prince are all good. Bad thoughts never even cross their minds. When the two fated good ones, Cinderella and the Prince, finally meet, only good can result. Further, since they live in a mythic reality where what they do now affects all of the future, they live "happily ever after." So, too, during wartime: *we* are good, *they* are bad, and when we defeat them, we too will live happily ever after.

* * *

In all my years in the army I was never taught that Communists were human beings. We were there to kill ideology carried by—I don't know—pawns, blobs, pieces of flesh. I was there to destroy Communism. We never conceived of old people, men, women, children, babies.

Lt. William Calley

In the mythic reality of wartime, statements of "our" bad qualities or "their" good ones are little tolerated. In World War II, we Americans only began to talk about "good Germans" after the war was over.

Looking at such changes in perception from a linguistic viewpoint, Abraham Myerson writes:

Men have died by the millions because of adjectives that became abstract nouns, so that a relatively good deed is Good, the disliked is Evil, and Sincerity and Faith are canonized even though there are sincere tigers and faithful Hindu thugs.

To clarify the last point Myerson makes here, I might point out that brave, faithful, and sincere members of the German SS died in Russia and in Normandy. This *does not in the least* change our opinion of the SS as completely evil. It was however, the bravery, faithfulness, and sincerity of the RAF pilots who defended Britain, and the American soldiers who died at Bataan and Anzio, that make us admire them. The same qualities are regarded as profoundly different when possessed by the good Us as opposed to the evil Them.

I do not mean, however, to imply that both sides in a war are always equally moral, and that therefore it does not matter which side wins: the nature of men like Hitler, and the reality of places like Dachau, indicate that there can be crucial differences. If those who fought—however bravely and sincerely—for Germany during World War II had won, the concentration camp would indeed have inherited the earth and the world would be profoundly worse than it is now. Similarly, the victory of Pol Pot and the Khmer Rouge made Cambodia into a country of horror. Both sides in a war perceive the other as evil; this does not change the fact that one may actually *be* evil.

Unless we are able to understand the larger picture of the perceived reality in which a war takes place, the behavior exhibited therein is incomprehensible. Konrad Lorenz demonstrates this point when he writes:

> . . . perfectly good natured men, who would not even smack a naughty child, proceed to be perfectly able to release rockets or to lay carpets of incendiary bombs on sleeping cities, thereby committing hundreds and thousands of children to a horrible death in the flames. The fact that it is good, normal men who did this is as eerie as any fiendish atrocity of war.

During a war, the division of the world into the forces of Good and the forces of Evil is so complete that not only similar qualities but also similar actions of the opposing sides are seen as fundamentally different. The World War II bombings of Rotterdam and of Hamburg are seen as two different *kinds* of behavior. ("They did it first" and "you must fight fire with fire"—as moral arguments—belong in a schoolyard, not any adult forum.)

In a mythic reality, words can no longer be relied on. The

enemy, being incapable of any good, always lie. They use words to conceal their true intentions, not to reveal them, as our side does (although it is all right for our side to lie in order to trick the enemy). No real communication is possible. Gandalf the White and the Dark Lord of Mordor (antagonists in the Tolkien saga *The Lord of the Rings*) really have nothing to say to each other beyond their attempts to trick or manipulate the other. Nor could Little Red Riding Hood, her Grandmother, and the Hunter have any real communication with the Wolf except that of deception and force. Since the Enemy has no regard for truth, negotiation is impossible. Once we have switched to a mythic view of reality, real talking stops. St. George and the dragon may talk, but it is meaningless; only the sword or claws and teeth will decide the issue.

* * *

To illustrate these ideas I have used some of the most familiar mythic-reality stories of our culture: *The Wizard of Oz, Cinderella, Little Red Riding Hood, The Lord of the Rings*. In all of these stories, as in most fairy tales and myths, there is a fundamental shift from the ordinary, sensory way of perceiving reality and in the action imperatives to which that perception leads. A new, fundamentally different way of perceiving, with very different implications for action, is presently arrived at and agreed on by a significant percentage of the group.

This is not a new idea; it has been stated in different ways by different people over the years. But it is important to realize that this concept is an integral part of understanding the process that leads to war, and that understanding this process will help us realize what specific actions we can take in order to abort it.

First, however, let us look at another description of this shift in perception. Erik Erikson writes of the "sudden total realignment" in perspective that takes place under certain conditions. This realignment, he says, may

> ... accompany conversion to the totalitarian conviction that the state may and must have absolute power over the lives and fortunes of its citizens ... [This is accompanied by] such

features as the exclusive focusing on a set of (friendly or unfriendly) affects on one person or idea, the primitivization of all affects thus focussed, and a Utopian (or cataclysmic) expectation of a total gain or a total loss to come from this focus . . .

Erikson believes that both the potential and the tendency to shift from sensory reality to mythic reality are very strong in human beings, and are only held back by the expenditure of large amounts of psychological energy—literally, by constant effort. This is an extremely important point that I shall explore later, both for its significance in making war such a popular activity and its implications for preventive action and education.

In early Christianity, the Manichean doctrine, which taught that existence is composed of two opposing forces, one totally pure and good and one totally evil, was regarded as a major heresy. Nevertheless, the Church was not above using the concept when it suited its purposes. When Pope Urban I called the First Crusade in 1095, he said three words that immediately changed the crusade from a sensory reality military problem to a mythic reality battle of heroic proportions: "God wills it." This call echoed throughout Europe and led not only to the deployment of trained military units, but also to such "magical" actions (illegitimate and stupid in sensory reality, but legitimate and intelligent in mythic reality) as the Children's Crusade and the many pogroms against Jewish communities in France, Germany, and Italy during that era.

During any war there are always a number of people on both sides who do not go along with the change from a sensory reality to a mythic reality. These people continue to recognize that war involves human beings killing other human beings, and that victory will not bring about a Utopia that will exist forever after. As more and more people *do* make this shift, however, the holdouts gradually realize that they must hold their tongues. When a critical percentage of any population has made such a shift, it becomes dangerous to challenge the now-accepted wisdom of mythic reality, and trying to do so is about as effective as trying to use logical arguments to dissuade a lynch mob. Of this type of exchange the philosopher George Santayana wrote: "There is nothing so helpless as reason when faced with unreason."

Sometimes fighting actually gets under way even without a critical percentage of citizens having made this shift. During the Vietnam War, few citizens believed they were living in heroic times, or that victory would change the world. They remained in the sensory reality, and—in this century at least—you cannot long maintain an effective war with that perspective. How our conflict with Vietnam ended is well known.

This change in perception of the structure of reality accounts for one phenomenon that has long puzzled students of war and human nature. War often inspires people to great heights of loyalty and self-sacrifice, and a willingness to suffer great hardship, injury, and even death. Certainly much of this heroic behavior can be traced to *esprit de corps*, but there is much more to it than that. Soldiers hasten to enlist in armies with little idea of the specific dangers they might face; often they and volunteer for transfer to very high-risk units, such as the commandos or the paratroopers. More than one's life is at stake here: great issues are being dealt with on the here-and-now plain of Armageddon.

The philosopher Alfred North Whitehead described this heroic behavior during World War II:

> As this war goes on and so many young men die before they have had time to live, I keep asking myself what it is that can inspire such heroism and devotion. . . . Manifestly most of these young men are not animated by complex political concepts. . . . Their ideas are multiform and . . . often conflicting. Yet there is one idea which they have in common, and while it isn't verbalized by them and while we have admitted there are no words for it, it is, as nearly as we can come to a definition, the idea of human worth. They are dying for the worth of the world.

THREE

Alternate Realities and Human Behavior

IN ORDER TO UNDERSTAND better how the use of alternate constructions of reality by human beings contributes to the perpetuation of war, it's important to have a better understanding of how these alternate realities work in day-to-day life. Let us consider a day in the life of an imaginary businessman. In this man's everyday work, as he sits at his desk, he exists in a construction of reality we all know very well. It is the form of reality we in the West ordinarily think of as the real one. It is the reality in which we tie our shoelaces, and design shoes; in which we purchase airplane tickets, and take taxis to airports. This businessman would say, as would most of us, that this is the only *real* reality, and that any other reality is actually some aberration or other, usually temporary. Since this construction is very highly influenced by the structure of our physical sensory apparatus, it can be called the sensory reality.

One evening, the businessman comes home after work. He knows there have been some cases of meningitis in the area, and he's worried about his four-year-old child. Arriving at home, he hears the child crying upstairs. As he goes upstairs, he is terribly frightened. He finds himself pleading, "Please, don't let it be meningitis." As he climbs the stairs he is really praying, and his whole consciousness is involved in this prayer. He is completely organized in such a way that this praying is the only thing that makes sense to him—what he is doing at that moment is the most reasonable thing to be doing. He does not question it. At that moment he is perceiving reality (and reacting to it) differ-

43

ently than he does during the rest of his regular day. At work he knows there would be absolutely no point to such pleading; the universe, as he ordinarily construes it, does not respond to emotion and prayer.

He arrives upstairs and finds to his vast relief that the child is not ill; she has only awakened upset and frightened. Holding the child in his arms, the father says soothingly, "It's all right." What is really happening here? The child is confused and frightened, and the businessman reassures her by saying, in effect, "It's all right. The universe is friendly. Things are all right." Now in his ordinary, everyday state of consciousness, the way he customarily organizes reality, this is certainly not true. He lives in a world where the passage of time will eventually result in the inevitable death and total annihilation of both him and his child. But one cannot say this to a child and also say, "It's all right, the universe is friendly."

But the businessman is not lying. At this moment he is in a completely different construction of reality than he was during the day or when he was coming up the stairs. Out of a deep sincerity he is saying, in effect, "There is a way of being in the universe where love transcends death and where the universe will not annihilate us." Again, he has organized reality in a different way. At this moment, this is what he *knows* to be the complete truth.

After reassuring and playing with his daughter, the businessman comes downstairs. That evening he and his wife go dancing. During the evening he is dancing in his usual way, enjoying it more or less, thinking of various things: the music, his partner, what they'd been talking about, other people, and so forth. Suddenly he realizes that for a period of time—he is not sure exactly how long—everything was different. During this period of time he wasn't thinking about anything. He was not in a daze. He was not in a trance. He was not asleep. As a matter of fact, he was very wide awake and alert, but his whole being was doing just one thing—dancing. After it was over, he felt good, "charged up," slightly "high," and very pleasantly relaxed. If that period is analyzed carefully, we find that once again he had been organizing reality in a different way. No longer was he listening *to* the music, dancing *with* his wife, *avoiding* the other people, but rather he and the music and his wife were, in a very fundamental sense, one. He was moving as if he were part of a network that included the music, the floor, the other people, and the whole scene. He was dancing far better than he ordinarily did. It was almost as if he and his wife had a kind of telepathy between them, responding to each other's movements and perceptions in a way far superior to their ordinary interaction. In the reality he was living at that moment there were no separations between things; all things flowed into each other.

Later that evening, at home, he and his wife sit listening to a Beethoven sonata. During many passages of the music, he again organizes the universe in a different way than he does during his ordinary workday. In this reality, it is not he who is listening to the music—he and the music are one; it is inside as much as it is outside him; he is not talking about it, he is not thinking about it, he is just intensely *being* with the music.

That night he goes to sleep, and during his sleep he has a dream. In the dream strange things happen. A kangaroo appears, hopping around the base of a mountain. Somehow it has the face of his older brother. He talks to it. The scene shifts and is then underwater. A beautiful mermaid appears. During the dream he does not question the "strange" things that happen. He knows they are right. He has again organized reality in a different way, a way in which all things are possible, all connections can be made; the symbol and the thing it symbolizes interact with each other constantly. This is yet another state of consciousness, another reality in which our businessman lives.

To use a modern phrase, the businessman was in an altered state of consciousness during these different incidents. An altered state of consciousness and an alternate reality are two different sides of the same coin. When I describe its rules and its "basic limiting principles" (to use a term of the twentieth-century philosopher C. D. Broad), I am talking about an alternate reality; when I am perceiving and reacting according to these rules, I am in an altered state of consciousness. Each of us, during each day, uses several different such constructions of the universe. We are in "altered states of consciousness," we are using "different metaphysical systems," we are in "alternate realities."

All the scientific evidence we have indicates that this shifting is essential to us. Certainly it is universal—it occurs in every culture and in every historical age we know of. If we encourage the use of alternate realities—as in those often achieved during meditation, play, listening to or playing serious music, and so forth—we increase the ability of human beings to reach new potentials. If we prevent the use of such alternate realities, we run the risk of incurring damage. This has been shown, for example, in the experimental work done on preventing people from dreaming while allowing them to have a normal amount of sleep. The research had to be discontinued because it caused psychological damage to the individuals being tested. One of the most fascinating things about alternate realities is that at the time you are using one it makes perfect sense to you, and you know it is the only correct way to view reality. It is only common sense.

Before exploring further the particular construction of reality used by a large percentage of the population in what we may call a "mythic war," and a smaller percentage in what we may call a "sensory war," let us look again for a moment at the day we have described in the life of our imaginary businessman. Certain aspects of this day seem particularly important.

First, in whatever construction of reality he is using, the businessman almost invariably believes it to be the true and only valid interpretation of reality. He does not question this assumption of its correctness. He is in a particular "dream" of the world, and while in a dream one usually does not wonder at or question its validity.

Second, the businessman moves fluidly and *expertly* from one mode to another. He knows how to do this even though he could not tell you how to do it or what he knows about the process. He goes from one construction to another as easily as an experienced European traveller, when crossing borders, shifts his language, gestures, money-counting techniques, ways of being civil, and many of his automatic small behaviors without thinking.

Finally, each mode is used appropriately according to the specific person's needs and the overall context of the situation. In the "unitary" mode, where the businessman reassures the child that "it's all right," and he perceives the universe as a seamless garment where love transcends all, he still may reach for a glass of water if the child coughs or if his own throat is dry; he still will stretch his legs if they feel a bit cramped, or cover the child with a blanket if the room seems chilly.

* * *

In other research carried out by the physicist-philosopher Henry Margenau and myself, it was useful to organize the major modes of construing reality used by human beings into four classes: the "sensory" mode, the "unitary" (or clairvoyant) mode, the "transpsychic" mode, and the "mythic" mode. This is not the place to describe these different modes in detail; a fuller picture of them is presented in our book, *Einstein's Space and Van Gogh's Sky.* However, it is useful to understand that the reality construction used in wartime is one subclass of what we have called the mythic mode.

In the mythic reality we never question *why* evil exists; it simply is. Cinderella's stepmother and the Dark Lord of Mordor simply are evil, as Cinderella and Gandalf are good. The enemy *is* evil and no psychoanalysis of the fact is necessary, relevant, or possible.

Since the enemy is evil and we are not, and since there is no "explanation" for this (e.g., we have not had childhood experiences which caused this difference), there is no reason not to starve, torture or kill them; after all, they cannot really be considered part of our own species. The World War II German generals treated the Russians with just such brutality; of 5.7 million Russians taken prisoner, 3.7 million died in German hands. The Japanese behaved similarly to their prisoners.

Hiroshima was picked as a target for the dropping of the first atomic bomb according to criteria laid down by James B.

Conant, who later became the president of Harvard University. Among these criteria were that the target area include a factory complex full of workers, surrounded by closely packed workers' housing. Some 80,000 people died in the bombing. Someone guided by a sensory reality orientation might well have picked a target featuring a factory complex *not* surrounded by closely packed workers' housing. However, the choice made is typical of what can be expected from even a highly intelligent, educated, decent man if he is using a mythical construction of reality.

The bombing of Dresden, which killed 135,000 people in twenty-four hours, was decided on a similar basis. From a sensory reality perspective it was useless, meaningless murder that did not bring the end of the war any closer. From a mythic reality viewpoint it was a good and correct decision. How our behavior shifts when we change from one reality mode to another is exemplified by Franklin Roosevelt's ordering a policy of strategic bombing during World War II—after he had written to all of the combatants at the outset of the war requesting them *not* to bomb cities.

Robert McNamara, secretary of defense during the Johnson Administration, called the bombing of North Vietnam "protective reaction air strikes." If the North Vietnamese had been able to bomb California (where supplies and troops were organized to be used against them), we would certainly have used different language to describe their efforts. In the mythic mode there are two separate sets of morals. Whether an act is good or evil depends on who does it—us or them. We kill and, for example, bomb civilian centers, in the service of peace and the general good of mankind. They do so because they are evil.

This is why soldiers often become so angry at the enemy when a comrade is killed. Logically there is little reason for their anger—we are at war in order to be able to kill them and vice versa. However, this anger is often very great, and not only because the lost comrade was loved; it is also because the enemy broke the rules. According to the unspoken but comprehended view of reality defined by the mythic mode, the good people (us) are supposed to kill the bad people (them), not the other way around. When a comrade (one of us) is killed, it is experienced as a violation.

Our tradition of judging different groups by completely different standards is very old. See, for example, the Homeric texts. The nobles are judged according to entirely differently criteria than those who are common-born. Achilles and Ulysses are very successful psychopaths, one very expert in killing, the other just as expert in devising tricks to get his way. Frankly, you would not want either of them about the house. But because they are born noble, their acts are judged as positive and praiseworthy in the *Iliad* and the *Odyssey*.

During wartime, not only are there two sets of morals that allow us to judge our "enemies" differently than ourselves and our allies, but also we never question this difference. It is seen as an inherent to this scheme of reality. It *is* justice. The Italian writer Ignazio Silone observed:

> What struck me most about the Russian Communists, even in such really exceptional personalities as Lenin and Trotsky, was their utter incapacity to be fair in discussing opinions that conflicted with their own. The adversary, simply for daring to contradict, at once became a traitor, an opportunist, a hireling. An *adversary* in good faith is inconceivable . . .

Part of the great attraction of Marxism for so many people was the fact that Marx gave us an intellectual justification to move into the mythic reality. The pure and just man (the worker) will lead us to "the end of history" and paradise (the classless society from which we all originally sprang). The attraction of Marxism's combination of a "scientific" view of history and a mythological universe, of nineteenth-century rationalism and heroic good-versus-evil struggle, is very strong. In Marx's world the worker is entirely good, and though he may be misled he will eventually triumph over the inherently and completely bad bourgeois and the totally evil and selfish capitalist. Cosmic forces are allied with the worker: "history fights on our side." And after the triumph of the good, we will all live happily ever after in a Golden Age. Here is an apparently rational and scientific approach to a great and noble cause—a mythic interpretation of reality—to live and die for. "This generation is manure for the next," the Bolsheviks of 1917 said of themselves. Small wonder that Winston Churchill called Marxism "an enchanted quagmire."

To use some well-known examples from popular culture, we see a sensory construction of reality used in the television series "Star Trek," in spite of its futuristic setting and imaginative characters and plots. There are no completely bad sentient beings. Reason can, and in nearly every episode does, lead to peace—peace for that problem at that time. By contrast, in the *Star Wars* movie series, a mythic mode is used. The good characters are all good and the bad ones all bad. Only superior force ultimately wins and, at the end, wins forever. The evil emperor is dead, his evil machines destroyed, his evil chief henchman (who was once good, but was misled—seduced by the Dark Side of the Force) redeems himself in death, and all the good people will clearly live happily ever after.

In the mythic orientation, the good people always emerge victorious. This is known by the combatants from the very beginning of the conflict, so that even defeats are seen as just ongoing action; and action, we know, will eventually lead to victory. When it was announced during World War II that General MacArthur had reached Australia after having retreated from the defeat/disaster of the Philippines with his whole army either dead or held prisoner by the Japanese, a taxi driver said to Margaret Mead:

> It just makes me feel good, it makes we want to go and enlist. I was in the last war and I think I'll get into this one. Makes you want to fight to hear about a man like that.

The mythic mode always leads to such extremes; there is no middle ground. The evangelist Jerry Falwell put it clearly: "The war is not between fundamentalists and liberals, but between those who love Jesus Christ and those who hate Him." "Liberals" and "fundamentalists" are sensory reality terms. Falwell is making sure that his followers perceive the conflict in mythic terms instead, so they have no doubt as to who is right and who is wrong.

Ruth Benedict describes the opposite sides in a war and how each sees the same situation. ". . . on the one side [us] it was a question of Divine Truth and the true believer, of revelation and of God; on the other [them] it was a matter of mortal error, of fable, of the damned and of devils."

In the mythic reality, force is ultimately the answer. The evil people are, by definition, totally evil and not redeemable by reason or sentiment. They can only be stopped by force, and a force often abetted by cunning. Even the rebel angels, according to Milton, had to be subdued by force. In this reality, the Sermon on the Mount must always devolve into the Church Militant. All mythic sequences of action or narrative (myths, stories, legends, and wars, when reality is constructed in the mythic mode) start with an act of will. They all end with the hero or heroes (or heroines) going on an adventure (usually leaving home to do so) and the successful appeal to arms.

Further, from the mythical perspective we can never be sufficiently prepared for conflict. Our defenses are never adequate to protect us from the forces of evil. The devil always has new weapons, new tricks. We can never be certain about conflict and so we *always* need a larger air force, more atomic bombs, and so on, without end.

A major problem with a mythical reality view of the world, then, is that those who hold it can never rest peacefully, since the results of any conflict they enter must inevitably fall short of their predictions and demands—which are the same. Since the "ideal Communist Man" hypothesized by Marx and Lenin never appeared, the Soviet Union had to go on killing or shipping off to the gulags all of the "enemies of the state"—the "kulaks," "traitors," "saboteurs" and what have you—until the system finally collapsed. The Nazis had to keep on expanding Germany's borders, and "purifying" their race, because no matter how much *Lebensraum* they had or how many Jews they killed, the new, ideal system they were striving for was not achieved.

During the sixties and early seventies, most of the countercultural communes in the United States ultimately failed, because no matter how much they worked, shared, gave, or smoked, they did not become the ideal community they were striving to be, nor did the ideal new human being appear. The Anabaptists of the Renaissance had to kill more and more Catholics and "heretics" the longer the New Jerusalem failed to come into existence. Orthodox Jews must keep on trying to influence the behavior of other Jews until the Messiah appears. Systems like these, based on a mythical reality evaluation, *must* keep on increasing their zeal and efforts, until their proponents collapse with exhaustion or are killed.

We all tend, as did our imaginary businessman, to use both mythic and non-mythic interpretations of reality, moving back and forth between them. The difference between a mythic war and a non-mythic, sensory war, is that in the mythic war such a large part of the population is using a mythic approach that the society "tips," and it becomes extremely unpopular or actually physically dangerous to express a sensory reality perspective. Thus, it becomes impossible for there to be any real shifting back and forth between the two different modes.

One of the fascinating aspects of the mythic construction of reality is the fact that it is usually applied to only two general areas: human behavior and interaction on the one hand, and the great forces of the cosmos on the other. It is not applied to *things*, to tools, implements, or other articles of everyday life. The most dedicated communists, the most fanatical Nazis, the most extreme religious fundamentalists all know that if they want certain types of food to be edible, the food must be cooked; that if those foods are left on the fire too long they will be burned; and so forth. In such dealings, they know that a sensory construction of reality holds true. We may regard the enemy as the great Satan and firmly believe that after he is defeated we will all live happily ever after, but we know that in order to wage war we must buy weapons, have cartridges that fit our rifles, and teach our gunners geometry so they can hit their targets. We are perfectly clear about how these two methods of construing reality relate to each other, and about when and where to use each. We may be going to a great crusade in God's name to make the world safe for democracy, but we drive on the correct side of the street to get there. "All my means are sane, my object and motives are mad," said Captain Ahab of his great mythic quest for Moby Dick.

* * *

Sometimes, however, when we need to influence events but do not know how to, we shift from the mythical construction of reality to the magical. This is another construction of reality widely used by human beings. The magical and mythical are quite different. In the mythical we try to invoke the great forces of the universe; in the magical we try to use the same systems to influence specific events.

A mariner finds his boat has been left stranded on the shore by a receding tide. He uses a book to look up a table of high and low tides that tells him exactly when he can expect the next high tide that will float his boat. Then he waits, with more or less patience, for the time to pass. Since he has sufficient sensory information to deal with the problem, he continues to use this mode of reality and his perceptions and reactions conform to it.

The same mariner, on his now-refloated sailboat, is some weeks later becalmed at sea. There is no wind and he does not have sufficient information to predict with any accuracy when the wind will again start to blow. He is, therefore, likely to shift to the magical mode of reality without being aware of it. Indeed, he would deny it or laugh ruefully at himself if you pointed it out to him. His behavior, however, shows this shift. He may whistle for a wind or put his hat on backward. Although he is not aware of what he is doing—and, if pressed, would say these actions are merely "superstitions"—he *acts* as if the world now were constructed on quite different lines than it was when he was stranded on the beach, when he would not even have thought of whistling for a quicker high tide.

The stranded mariner is a trivial example, yet his behavior can show how easily and naturally we can shift our conceptions of reality. If my car stops running in the middle of a deserted country road, I will first see if I have enough data in the sensory reality to fix it. Since I know little about cars, this testing will probably consist of tapping the gas gauge to see if it has gotten stuck, opening the hood to see if there are any loose wires I can notice, and possibly removing the gas feed tube and blowing through it to make sure it is clear. (This last once actually worked for me!) If none of these procedures suffice, I have then run out of *sensory* information with which I can deal with the situation.

Without noticing what I am doing, I may then make a shift to another reality mode. I might kick the car several times as if it were a stubborn donkey I could persuade to move in this way. I might promise it a complete motor tune-up and perhaps even a new paint job if it will only behave. Presently, I may threaten to sell it to the nearest junkyard unless it behaves and gets going *this minute*. And so on. In my frustration over not being able to use the sensory reality satisfactorily, I have, unawares, shifted the entire way I construe reality. Again, as with the becalmed mariner, it is my behavior that bears this out. In my actions, I have behaved exactly like the natives of the Trobriand Islands. When they go on a routine fishing expedition where they are familiar with all of the variables operating, they are only concerned that their canoes, paddles, and fishing gear are in order. When they are going on a more hazardous trip into unfamiliar waters, where they do not know all of the variables involved, they avail themselves of incantations, magical rituals, and amulets. In a magical reality, we also believe in the special power *things* may have. An amulet will protect me from evil forces; a weapon (e.g., King Arthur's Excalibur) will make me invulnerable in battle. A "lucky hat" will insure good fishing.

I have described this shift to the magical mode at some length because, in theory at least, the mythic and magical modes are often confused. This makes understanding what is actually going on in a particular situation much more difficult. In practice, this difference is well understood, particularly by the military; we do not hear anymore the major complaint of the eighteenth- and nineteenth-century African tribesman that the witch doctor's chants and unguents did not deflect the white soldiers' bullets. A more recent example of confusion between these two modes came during the period of antiwar protests over the U.S. involvement in Vietnam, when a group of protesters tried—more than half-seriously—to discomfit the military establishment by levitating the Pentagon. However, except for odd occurrences of this sort, the confusion tends to be more in theory than fact. We are too expert in shifting from one construction of reality to another to make this kind of error very often.

* * *

In this chapter I have tried to give a general idea of how we use different constructions of reality at different times and in different situations. This is meant only as an introduction to a concept which has been widely explored elsewhere, in many different fields. Any textbook of modern physics, for example, will make it clear that physicists need to employ different constructions of reality for the too-small-to-see-even-theoretically (quantum physics) and the too-large-or-fast-to-see-even-theoretically (relativity physics) than they employ to explain the material and data within the range of our senses.

The same situation looks completely different when a different construction of reality is used to look at it. An analogy might be made (following the example of the semanticist Alfred Korzybski) to the different sorts of maps available for a particular area. Let us imagine two maps of the area around New York City. One is that which the pilot of a small private plane might use on a clear day. He looks down from his airplane and sees rivers, bridges, and buildings, and knows from these landmarks where he is and how to get to the airport. The other map is the one the pilot of a commercial airliner will generally use. This map shows radio beacons only. These are two different maps of what is "out there," existing in the same geographical space but without a single feature in common. We could make the point further by imagining other kinds of maps of the same area, such as barometric maps, population density maps, soil sample maps, or what have you. Each would show a different picture, contain different entities, lead to different behavior, and be useful for accomplishing different goals. None of these, however, is the *true* or *correct* map of the New York City area.

This is not the place to develop this concept in detail. However, it *is* very important for an understanding of war. A shift by an appreciable portion of a nation's population into the particular construction of reality widely used during wartime makes war very likely to commence; sometimes such a shift makes war inevitable, and in every case it makes war very hard to stop.

However, a few other comments on this way of construing the mythic reality mode in warfare may be helpful here. First, it is very tempting for human beings to move into the mythic mode. Such students of human behavior as Ernst Cassirer and Erik Erikson have pointed out that this tendency is a part of our human potential, and that it takes energy and effort *not* to revert to this mode. It is harder and less comfortable to use a sensory reality evaluation in stressful situations. The simplicity, the belief that we are on the side of personal and cosmic good, the faith in an assured outcome—all make the mythic view of reality much more comfortable than the common-sense sensory view. In Arthur Miller's words, "It is much more reassuring to see the world in terms of totally innocent victims and totally evil instigators . . . " Lis Harris wrote in *The New Yorker* about the Hasidim, a group who have an essentially mythic view of reality:

> I envied them their sureness and the sheer weight it gave them. I had, of course, my family, my friends, my work, and the various pleasures that came my way, but spiritually, I felt as if I floated weightlessly in the universe. The Hasidim had a world without time, eternal life, and the extraordinary sense that everything they did counted.[16]

Even those who understand the danger of slipping into the mythic mode are vulnerable under conditions of pressure. George Orwell wrote of the intellectual left wing during the Spanish Civil War:

> The thing that was truly frightening about the war in Spain was . . . the immediate reappearance in left wing circles of the mental atmosphere of the Great War. The very people who for twenty years sniggered over their own superiority to war hysteria were the ones who rushed straight back into the mental slum of 1915.

Second, the shift to the mythic mode in difficult times not only reduces our sense of stress, it also creates a sense of certainty, a joyfulness and an optimism. We feel good about ourselves. Arthur Koestler, writing of the moment almost immediately after he accepted the communist viewpoint:

> I was already reaping the reward of all conversions, a blissfully clear conscience. . . . something had clicked in my brain which shook me like a mental explosion. To say that one had 'seen the light' is a poor description of the mental rapture which only the convert knows (regardless of the faith he has been converted to). The new light seems to pour from all directions across the skull; the whole universe falls into a pattern like the stray pieces of a jigsaw puzzle assembled by magic at one stroke. There is now an answer to every question, doubts, conflicts are a matter of the tortured past—a past already remote, when one had lived in dismal ignorance in the tasteless, colorless world of those who *don't know*. Nothing henceforward can disturb the convert's inner peace and serenity—except the occasional fear of losing faith again . . .

Finally, the fantasy-like viewpoint of the mythic mode is optimistic. No matter how tremendous the odds, good will triumph over evil. *We* expect to win because we see ourselves as representing the forces of good. Once a large percentage of a nation's citizens has taken on the mythic perspective, they will not be willing to surrender until a defeat is clear, immediately present, and overwhelming. We become joyous and excited. We look forward to the war as a high and wonderful adventure that we are all in together.

> . . . no one can read the newspapers or letters written in the first year of that war [1914] without being impressed by the alacrity, dedication and even the joy with which every nation of Europe threw itself into that meat grinder.

Our great cause, which gives such meaning to our life, leads not only to optimism and joy, but also to an ecstatic and dedicated sense of being. In florid and overblown terms, a southern lady wrote in her diary in 1861 a verse which expresses this sentiment clearly:

> Their bosom they bared to the glorious strife
> and their oaths were recorded on high—
> To prevail in the cause that was dearer
> than life
> or crushed in its ruins to die.

Even a poet of the high caliber of Walter de la Mare could write about the English dead in the filthy trench warfare of World War I:

> Nay, nay, sweet England, do not grieve!
> Not one of these poor men who died
> But did within his soul believe
> That death for thee was glorified.

FOUR

Mythic and Sensory Wars

If you turned Hell upside down you would find "Made in Germany" stamped on the bottom.

Billy Sunday (1917)

This is the Mother of all wars. It is led by the Satan, Bush.

Saddam Hussein (1991)

Both sides claim to be acting according to the will of God.

Abraham Lincoln (1862)

FINDING USEFUL ANSWERS to problems in any field means working between two different extremes of thought. On one side is H. L. Mencken's maxim, "To every complex problem there is a simple answer. And it is always wrong." On the other is the science fiction writer Poul Anderson's law: "There is no problem, however difficult and complex, but that looked at from the right angle can be made more difficult and complex."

No simple answer to the problem of preventing war is sufficient. But answers that are too complex will not be helpful in our search for useful ways to curb a prospective war. Most social scientists whom I have approached concerning this question over the past twenty years have told me that the question of war's causes was not a legitimate area for research because of one of two reasons. The first reason was that they already knew the answer, and that answer amounted to some simple, single factor ("displacement of aggression," "human greed," "territoriality," or perhaps a specific culprit). The second reason was that the problem was too complex to answer at all. Both groups agreed that the problem of war was not amenable to social science research.

In order to avoid both the overcomplex and the oversimple way of looking at war's causes, it seems necessary to divide

59

wars into two general and sometimes overlapping classes. This division appears to fit the data, at least for the last 150 years of armed conflict—roughly from the Crimean War to the present.

* * *

The way the general population experienced and reacted to war changed dramatically about the time of the Crimean War. Before that time wars were generally regarded as distant affairs fought by glorious Homeric warriors for a noble (ours) or evil (theirs) cause. News of the fighting came to the general populace slowly and with many delays.

The invention of the foreign correspondent, the newspaperman-on-the-scene, in the 1830s, and then the development of the telegraph in the 1840s, changed all that. Now the public could really be involved in a war; suddenly, a "you-are-there" possibility presented itself. *And the public showed that it wanted to be involved.* The desire for news of foreign wars was overwhelming—if, however, it was news that made the fighting men and the conflict itself appear heroic. The fresher the news, and the greater the mythic character it gave our men in the fray, the more newspapers it sold. Soon an unfortunate feedback loop developed. The more these mythic characteristics appeared in its war reports, the more a particular newspaper sold; therefore, the more often newspapers printed such reports. Other, more objective types of reporting were clearly not welcome. William Howard Russell (the greatest foreign correspondent of the period), working for the London *Times*, was hounded out of America after he accurately reported how Union soldiers panicked and ran at Bull Run. When he reported, also accurately, what the war in the Crimea had actually been like on the front, the *Times* was barred from the gentlemen's clubs in London.

Technology had made it possible for the public to feel more actively engaged in war than ever before. The public grabbed this opportunity with enthusiasm, and its appetite for new was eagerly exploited by the press. War of the mythic variety was the greatest single way ever discovered to sell newspapers. When a war was not of the mythic kind, however—when a majority of the citizens had not decided it was a good-against-evil battle where the fate of the cosmos was at stake—reports of that war did not sell newspapers to anything like the same degree. The wars waged by the U.S. in Korea and Vietnam were examples of these less popular conflicts, not viewed in mythic terms by a majority of the population.

Most of the photographs taken during the Civil War were not published until long afterward. They showed all too clearly that it was neither *dulce* nor *decorum* to *pro patria mori*—it was neither sweet nor fitting to die for one's country. Similarly, the siege of Mafeking during the Boer War was seen as a glorious and heroic stand by General Baden-Powell and the British forces. The London *Times* refused to publish accounts by its own correspondent that the British had been so successful because of Baden-Powell's food policy—letting the black inhabitants of Mafeking starve while he provided food to the whites. Because this information was suppressed, Baden-Powell (who later went on to found the Boy Scouts) and the other "heroic defenders" could become heroes to the British public.

In order for a war to retain its mythic aspects, and thus increase the intensity of meaning in our lives and bond us more completely as group members, enough of the real facts of how war is waged must be concealed. Any information that lessens war's psychological assets is generally rejected. For instance, although it was known to many people, and obvious to war correspondents, no newspaper published the agreement of the Allied and German high commands not to use aerial bombardment against each other's headquarters during World War I.

In World War II, China was seen as our brave and suffering ally. No public mention was made of the fact that it had a terribly corrupt government (the Kuomintang, led by Chiang Kai-shek) far more concerned with lining the pockets of its officials, and stockpiling the weapons we sent them for later use against the Communists, than it was with fighting the Japanese. This corruption was so widely known to our government officials, the press, and to most of our soldiers in the area, that the historian Barbara Tuchman has called the situation "The China Hoax."

In the opening months of the Persian Gulf War, there was absolutely no mention in the press, nor in the very frequent TV news and "analysis" programs, of such facts as that one of our allies, Syria, had recently destroyed the party opposing its ruling group by ringing the city of Hama with troops and artillery and razing it; 30,000 were killed in the bombardment. Nor was there mention of the fact that both Saudi Arabia and Syria are in a state of war with Israel, having consistently refused—for over 40 years—to discuss a truce, let alone a peace treaty, or even to recognize the right of Israel to exist. Nor of the fact that in Arabic, the word for "black person" (*iswid*) and the word for "slave" are still the same.

After the Persian Gulf War was over, NBC news commentator John Chancellor wrote in the *New York Times* (April 1, 1991):

> From the very beginning, millions of people were ready to believe anything bad about Saddam Hussein. . . . Accounts of Iraqi atrocities were accepted without question. There was the tale of premature babies thrown out of incubators in a Kuwait hospital and left to die. It never happened. . . .

> Before the fighting began, the press reported breathlessly that Iraq might actually use fuel-air explosives, a horrible weapon of almost nuclear potency. When the fighting began, the country that did use fuel-air explosives was the U.S., and nobody complained.

During World War II, Captain Colin Kelly was widely reported to be a great American hero for sinking a Japanese battleship by diving his airplane down her funnel. He never actually did this, but we needed a hero and the story was useful at the time. When the Japanese began using kamikaze tactics toward the end of the war, however, Kelly's name abruptly disappeared from public mention. After all, if Kelly was a hero for what he had done, then so were the Japanese suicide pilots, and we could not have that.

Neither during the Persian Gulf War, nor in the months following its end, was there any great mention in the media of the fact that Syria demanded (and obtained) $3 billion as the price of sending troops to Saudi Arabia and serving as one of the allies of the United States in the "coalition" forces. Nor has there been serious mention of the fact that once Desert Storm had begun, Syria refused to let its forces be sent into combat. The $3 billion was promptly spent on armaments, particularly Chinese missiles of the "Scud" variety.

Even now, with the Persian Gulf War ended and the American soldiers returned home, we still know relatively little about the negative side of the war. It was the most "sanitized" war since Crimea. We saw it on television every day and night, framed as a war of "smart bombs" finding their way unerringly down the ventilator shafts of Iraqi strongholds; but there was never a picture, and scarcely a mention, of the human beings who had been inside those defenses.

Even the pictures of the tremendous slaughter our planes wreaked on the Iraqis fleeing Kuwait showed only mile after mile of wrecked vehicles. One got the impression the vehicles had driven themselves over that fatal highway. No bodies were photographed. The only radio or TV program of which I am aware that discussed how large a percentage of our bombs missed military and hit civilian targets while the war was going on was "Perspective" on ABC Radio. Anyone could listen to it and get this information—anyone, that is, who was awake and listening at 5:00 A.M. on Sunday mornings!

* * *

Since the development of the foreign correspondent and the telegraph line, then, and the change in the Western world's approach to war that came with them, it is possible to fit wars into two general, sometimes overlapping, classes. There are wars in which there is a large mythic element in the way a majority of the citizens evaluate the situation (mythic wars), and there are wars in which the mythic viewpoint is taken only by a few, and the majority retain a sensory perspective of the conflict (sensory wars).

It is worthwhile noting again here that *all* wars are brought about—and bring about—a shift from the sensory reality evaluation system to that of the mythic reality. The psychological

63

forces moving us in this direction are strong even at the most peaceful of times. (Arthur Deikman, in his important book *The Wrong Way Home*, has shown how much of the mythic structure of reality exists even in the course of our everyday lives.)

It's crucial to understand that the difference between a mythic and a sensory war is always a matter of degree: what percentage of a nation's population sees a war as a means of permanently solving all of their problems? For citizens of the United States, the experience of World War II was an excellent example of a mythic war. From the beginning of our participation the differences between "us" and "them" were quite clear. We, for example, had submarines, and they had U-boats; there was never any question about how different these were. Ours sank only warships, while theirs attacked unarmed civilian ships and hospital ships at every opportunity (and lay in wait looking for others). Ours were manned by intrepid officers who were deeply concerned about the survival of their crews, and who knew a lot about both the ideals we were fighting for and the evil we were fighting. Our crews were composed of individuals who were very brave in the face of terrible danger. (In the movies, sub crews always had one sailor from Brooklyn, one from the far West or South, and one old salt who had been a submariner for a long time. The officers were all WASPs.) Our submarines bravely sailed uncharted waters, confronting danger for the sake of saving the future.

The enemy's U-boats were manned by cold, devious, unimaginative officers who never worried about the safety of their men or about the ideals they were fighting for. They skulked along the sea bottoms waiting for helpless enemy ships to come into sight of their periscopes. All the crew was cut from the same mold as the officers, except the crew were less intelligent.

Woe betide any American writer or commentator who did not keep up with the shift from a sensory orientation to a mythical one. He could face trouble in much the same way as Russian writers who, under Stalin, did not read the latest edition of *Pravda* and maintain the correct viewpoint of the moment. John Steinbeck wrote *The Moon Is Down* after the majority of the

American public had made the shift from a sensory to a mythic perception of World War II. In the book he showed German soldiers occupying a Norwegian town as human beings with human emotions. For this he was widely attacked and strongly vilified. He simply had not realized that Germans were now monsters and must feel and do only what monsters felt and did.

One aspect of this shift in orientation is the language people use. Countries become single organisms. There are fewer and fewer individual "Germans" or "Japanese"; there is only "Germany" or "Japan." No longer is there any division of opinion in the "enemy" country, with a decision being made there despite internal dissent. There is now simply one organism acting out of evil motive. It is no longer "The government of X, with the y party dissenting, decided to. . ." It is now "X did thus and so."

Individuals lose their individuality and uniqueness, becoming indistinguishable from the mass national identity. A derogatory nickname appears for the enemy, and we find it is far easier to kill a "Nip" or a "Kraut" than it is to kill a "Japanese" or a "German." They all become one and the same, including women and children; this is an aspect of their essential inhumanity, making it easier to kill them without feeling as if we were committing murder.

Reviewing any newspaper published during the period just before a war will show this change. All members of the opposition become the same—bad; they lose their distinctness. This is one difference between "us" and "them"—we may all be uniformly good and positive, but we also retain individual differences. "They" do not. In World War II, we saw our British allies as unique individuals. They were women working in the underground air control rooms directing fighter pilots to the locations of enemy bombers; they were Cockney soldiers, and soldiers from the farms; they were brave fire wardens, and officers from Eton and Cambridge, and Mrs. Miniver and Mr. Miniver. All were dedicated and good. However, there was no mention in American newspapers of the well-known fact that the Blitz produced a large class of skilled corpse robbers, who were frequently the first on the scene when a bomb hit a shelter; or the fact that when the Normandy invasion started, British jails and detention centers were full, and there were anti-Semitic graffiti on the walls of many English cities.

This change in the perception of reality generally begins, in the thinking of those involved, with a shift in definition: suddenly, a group of individuals living in a foreign geographical area become an enemy "country" acting as a single organism. An example of this (not really very extreme when compared with newspaper accounts from the same period), can be found in an entry in Kaiser Wilhelm II's personal diary in 1914, shortly before the assassination of the Archduke Ferdinand at Sarajevo:

> The net has been suddenly thrown over our head and England sneeringly reaps the brilliant success of her persistently anti-German world policy, against which we have proven ourselves helpless, while she twists the noose of our political and economic destruction out of our fidelity to Austria, as we squirm isolated in the net.

There are a number of special features differentiating mythic wars from sensory wars. Although distinguishing these two types is a matter of degree, real differences do emerge, as shown in the table following:

Mythic Wars	Sensory Wars
All classes of society fight in combat.	The lower economic classes and professional soldiers strongly predominate in combat.
There are widely sung songs about the war.	There are no such songs.
Widely known heroes appear.	There are few or no widely known heroes.
War is entered into with a sense of excitement and feelings of high energy.	War is entered into soberly and with a sad and regretful feeling.
There is a general belief that after the war is over (won), everything	The general belief is that after the war things will be pretty much as

will be different and better. We will move into a new and better period of history.

they were before it started. We will be in the same period of history.

Negative information about ourselves or our allies is suppressed.

Negative information about ourselves or our allies is widely known.

Antiwar activists are suppressed. No antiwar movements are tolerated.

Antiwar movements openly exist.

There is a general sense of this war being a crusade against evil.

There is no sense of a "good against evil" war, but rather a sense of a specific problem that must be solved.

If we compare the American mythic wars, such as World Wars I and II and the Civil War on the one hand, with the sensory wars in Korea and Vietnam on the other, the differences are clear. All classes of society fought in combat in the first group; from a statistical viewpoint, the situation was quite different in Korea and Vietnam. We are all familiar with songs from our mythic wars—"Mine Eyes Have Seen the Glory," "Dixie," "Tenting Tonite," "Over There," "Long Long Trail Awinding," "Praise the Lord and Pass the Ammunition," "Lili Marlene," "Bluebirds Over the White Cliffs of Dover," and many others. No such songs are remembered from Korea or Vietnam. We entered the mythic wars with excitement and almost a sense of joy. (On April 6, 1917, the audience at the New York Metropolitan Opera broke into long and loud cheers when the announcement was made that the U.S. had entered the war.) No such feelings were evident in the sensory wars. Nor were they evident when we entered the Persian Gulf War. During World War I (also known as the Great War, or The War to End All Wars), the Civil War, and World War II, we felt that the high crusade we had entered on would lead us to a new way of life. Things would be different. There was no such general feeling in the Korean or Vietnam conflict—just as, for that matter, there was no such feeling among the Soviet people during the USSR-Afghanistan conflict.

There were many well-known heroes from the mythic wars: Lee, Grant, Stonewall Jackson, Sergeant York, Eddie Ricken-backer, Blackjack Pershing, Hindenburg, The Red Baron, Patton, Marshal Zhukov, Rommel, and Eisenhower (military heroes often make a successful entry into politics after mythic wars, far less often after sensory wars). These heroes remain larger than life in our perception. There was certainly just as much heroism and inspired leadership in Korea, Vietnam, and Afghanistan, but which heroes of those wars are similarly remembered?

The antagonists in any conflict may not be perceiving the same kind of war: one may be evaluating the situation as a mythic war, the other as a sensory war. The U.S. actions in Korea and Vietnam, and the USSR-Afghanistan conflict come quickly to mind. The same situation existed in the Persian Gulf War. Certainly those perceptions may change. In the first six months of World War II, when many were still referring to it as the "the phony war," the general population of France saw the war with a sensory orientation. This changed after the Blitzkrieg.

Generally speaking, the more actual combat soldiers have seen, the more their viewpoint tends to shift from mythic to sensory. They are forced by the exigencies of the sensory reality, which is necessary for staying alive, to give up more and more of their mythic perceptions. They see opposing soldiers as similar to themselves and the enemy dead as similar to the dead on their own side. Similarly, military professionals more often have a sensory reality view of the tools of their trade—weapons, and their values and limitations—than do civilians. They also tend to have a much more common-sense, sensory reality view of war than do civilians, although this is by and large not unaccepted today. In 1982, all of the Joint Chiefs of Staff strongly supported reduction in our strategic nuclear arsenal. Their proposal was vetoed by a civilian, Defense Secretary Caspar Weinberger.

It is also important to note that bad news from the front, such as news of losses and of defeat, is far less demoralizing to those perceiving a mythic war than to those perceiving a sensory war. In a mythic war, bad news tends to increase people's determination, rather than decrease it as it does in a sensory war. This difference lasts until the final stages of defeat, when the mythic perception is abandoned and attention is turned instead to individual and family survival.

An extensive and beautifully written discussion of the mythic orientation as it affected people in World War II, and how the media encouraged and exploited that orientation, is presented in Paul Fussell's *Wartime*. I have learned much from this book and recommend it strongly to anyone interested in this area.

FIVE

War and the Psychological Needs of the Individual

The Human Heart is the starting point of all matters pertaining to war.

Marechal de Saxe,
Reveries on the Art of War, 1731

Son, when you are trying to stop wars, psychology is the only business you are in.

Philip Wylie, *Opus 21*

The people on Fieldstone Road in Wellesley, Massachusetts, celebrated the bombing of Pearl Harbor with an enormous party. Of course the families there were well aware that war is a terrible thing and they kept saying that to each other, but they were excited, even exalted because hate for a common enemy who is a long way away can make people feel almost ennobled. The radio did not make anything clear, except that the United States had been wantonly attacked and was going to war. "We're off!" Mark Kettel said, as though the war were a horse race or a long-awaited trip.

The first thing most of the people on Fieldstone Road did was to telephone all their relatives. Families gathered. Neighbors came in, drinks were mixed, and within a few hours the street looked as though a wedding, not a war, were being celebrated in every house.

Sloan Wilson, *Ice Brothers*

THE FIRST MODERN RESEARCH PROJECT I know of that asked the question "Why do men go to war?" was started by the United States Army in 1916. When news of it reached General Pershing, he ordered the study discontinued. He said

71

that the answer was obvious. "Men go to war," he said, "because they enjoy it."

Indeed, we cannot completely ignore this answer. (Bertrand Russell phrased it, "Many are happier in war than in peace.") War is just too omnipresent and constant a phenomenon to dismiss it out of hand. According to Adlai Stevenson, in the twenty years following World War II there were more than twenty wars in which national armies actively engaged in hostilities with each other. In the relatively peaceful year of 1970, the world had over 16 million men under arms. A study by the social psychologist Pitirim Sorokin showed that since 901 A.D., Russia has been at war for at least forty-six out of every hundred years, England fifty-six, Spain even more. Whatever other causes there may be, there is definitely *something* about war that appeals to human beings.

We have known how terrible war is at least since 416 B.C., when Euripides' *The Trojan Women*, the greatest antiwar play ever written, was first produced. The Athenians were deeply moved by it, so moved that they realized they had to do something in response. At the time they were in the midst of a long armed conflict. However, no peace movement followed the production; instead, there was a vote to drive the author, one of the most admired men of the period, into exile. It was a typical response toward peacemakers when the citizens of a nation are at war.

There is no particular plot to *The Trojan Women*—just a deep understanding of the effect of war. Euripides took Homer's *Iliad* (a story known well by every Greek) and its tale of glorious fighting by heroic men over the most beautiful woman in the world, and in his hands it turns into a story of a little group of women sitting in the square of their burned city, with their men dead and their children being killed in front of their eyes, waiting to be taken into permanent slavery. They talk of how war seems to them.

It was clear, superbly written, seen by everyone who was anyone in Athens, and ignored. No peace movement followed.

* * *

In the last three chapters I have explored the relation between war and the ways we construe or organize reality. The shift I have discussed here plays a major role in the human readiness to accept the sacrifices, privations, and dangers of war. The frequency of war, particularly in the last century, is not comprehensible otherwise.

Further, as every student of this transition (since the philosopher Friedrich Schelling first described the mythic orientation in the early nineteenth century) has pointed out, the shift into the mythic reality is natural and easy for human beings. It has also been stressed by many, from Ernst Cassirer to Erik Erikson, that it takes energy *not* to shift our perspective this way, and that particularly in times of stress and uncertainty there is a strong pull toward making this shift in the human consciousness.

However, there is much more to understanding our readiness to go to war. War satisfies, or promises to satisfy, other psychological needs. In this chapter I will discuss these needs under four different headings. These categories refer to certain almost universal human tendencies, present in all of us to a greater or lesser degree and varying during different periods of our lives.

Although it is necessary for the sake of clarity to distinguish between these different aspects of war's appeal, they often overlap and reinforce each other. We human beings do not have sharp dividing lines that mark where "displacement of aggression" stops and "need to be part of a group" begins. In reality our motivations are never absolutely separate, but in order to comprehend them clearly we need first to discuss them as if they were. As the sociologist-historian Tocqueville said, "Only God does not need categories."

The four elements of human motivations toward war are:

1. Displacement of aggression.
2. Projection of self-doubts and self-hatred.
3. Lack of meaning and purpose in life.
4. A need for greater belonging to a group.

(Since the first two of these aspects have already been so widely discussed as causes for intergroup hostility, I will present them only briefly here.)

Displacement of Aggression

A terrible, persistent religious war is going on in Northern Ireland. A Pakistani soldier in the British Army stationed there told the psychiatrist Robert Coles:

> These people hate each other. You are right. But they would become brothers overnight if 500 or 1,000 Pakistanis like me came to settle in Belfast—brothers under the skin.

Human beings have long known that if we displace our hostility, distancing it from those close to us (psychologically or physically), our life becomes much easier. We are surrounded by more good feelings and stronger groups. The Arab saying goes, "The enemy of my enemy is my friend," and the colloquial modern phrasing is, "Friends are acquaintances who have the same enemy." With someone to hate outside the group, interpersonal stresses are eased; the more enthusiastically we feel and express hostility toward those outside the group, the more accepted we are by—and the more enthusiastic we feel about—those in the group.

When Saul Alinsky wrote his handbook for social activists, *Reveille for Radicals*, he advocated a technique that intuitive leaders of groups have known for millennia. There will be times, said Alinsky, when there is tension and conflict in the group that threatens to tear it apart. He advised the leader to "keep a fight in the bank," to have an enemy in reserve so that, in times of tension, the group's angers and hostilities can be focused elsewhere and the group cohesion maintained, and usually even increased.

We feel much more at home with our neighbors and friends when we share a common enemy: the tensions between us are drained off and we become close comrades-in-arms. During the time Israel was under missile attack during the Persian Gulf War, *Hadassah* magazine asked Israelis to write letters about their feelings and experiences. The first two of these letters (and they were typical of those received) were as follows:

I have three kids under nine and to be honest I find them a bit of a handful—even in normal times. And now, since the missile attacks began and there's been no school, it seems that all they do is shriek and fight.

But Saddam Hussein and his Scuds can do with them what I can't. The moment the siren sounds they're three different kids. The game or the quarrel stops at once. They file off quickly to their sealed room. Each gets his gas mask out of his box. The boxes are always lined up in the same order, so that the little one, who can't read yet, knows where hers is. The masks go on, our big boy checking that his sisters have got theirs right. And peace reigns inside our home, if not outside it, until the all clear sounds.

And:

The Central Jerusalem Post Office isn't one of Israel's pleasanter experiences. The clerks are normally taciturn and surly, the lines long and the people impatient. Which was why the contrast struck me so strongly when I went in to pay my phone bill during the second week of the war. The waiting lines of the people were cheerful and talkative. The man behind the counter smiled at me. Not a single person tried to push in with 'just a quick question.' And waiting time seemed somehow shorter as we amateur strategists exchanged views on what Saddam would do next, what the allies ought to do, and how to win the war.

An Israeli, interviewed on American television during this period, said:

Israelis have become so much more polite to each other. There is friendliness, 'please' and 'thank you.' It is a wonderful feeling.

One of the major mistakes of the world's military up to and through World War II was a psychological one, concerning the effectiveness of bombing on civilian populations. Military planners consistently "failed to foresee that the direct involvement of civilian populations in warfare would *strengthen* [italics mine] their spirit and social cohesion." Populations were not driven to their knees by bombing, as was predicted, but became stronger and more unified. Both the German and Allied civilian bomb-ings demonstrated this. It is important to note that there were few psychological casualties during the period when civilian centers were being bombed. All the predictions of such damage were too high, often by a factor of twenty. Clearly, bombing actually strengthens a civilian population. It solves the "us-them" problem. Further, in World War II ". . . strategic bombing strengthened morale in the enemy soldiers and did not seriously affect war production."

Projection of Self-Doubts and Self-Hatreds

> Shame to him whose cruel striking
> Kills for faults of his own liking.
> Shakespeare, *Measure for Measure*, Act 1, Scene 2

It has been widely accepted in psychiatric and psychological circles that war is so widespread and popular because it offers a way to redirect our anxieties to a more comfortable target.

The psychiatrist Karl Menninger wrote:

> War . . . is a reflection of multiple . . . miniature wars in the hearts of individuals. . . . The war of nations is a magnification of the war of human motives . . .

A psychotherapist reported the following case history to me:

> "J" had always been an extremely anxious person. All his adult life he was rarely free of anxiety for an hour. The anxiety was "free-floating," going from one object and one possibility to another. It was constantly with him. As soon as World War II had started and the draft was instituted, the situation changed. During the war he worried only each morning about whether he would be drafted that day. He was in severe psychic pain until the daily mail was delivered. Once it had and the dreaded draft notice had not arrived, he felt fine the rest of the day and evening. Only the next morning did the pain resume. He had found a "hanger" on which to pin his anxiety and his life, until the birthday when he became too old to be drafted, was the best it had ever been. After that birthday, he resumed the pattern of anxiety in nearly all waking moments.[16]

When we find an outside source for our unacceptable feelings, drives, and wishes, our tension is greatly decreased. It is the enemy who is evil and to be rejected, not ourselves. "We crave scapegoats; targets to absorb our self-doubts, our feelings of worthlessness and hopelessness," wrote the psychiatrist Robert Coles.

Projection is an extremely useful way to rid ourselves of intrapersonal tensions. Instead of feeling bad about ourselves, we feel good as we go out to rid the world of evil. The words of the cartoon character Pogo ring true: "We have met the enemy and he is us."

Lack of Meaning and Purpose in Life

If the admiralty courted war like a mistress, if as the drum beat to quarters, the sailors came gaily out of the forecastle—it is because a fight is a period of intense and multiplied experience . . .

Robert Louis Stevenson

Without any meaningful goal except continuing the same rounds of activity, our inner life decays and we lose our purpose. War holds out the promise of our being needed in a great cause. As William James said:

All the qualities of a man acquire dignity when he knows that the service of the collectivity that owns him needs them. If proud of the collectivity, his own pride rises in proportion. No collectivity is like an army for nourishing such pride.

Bruce Catton, the historian of the Civil War, describes Decoration Day ceremonies in the town he grew up in:

The old men, simply because they were veterans of the Civil War, gave a color and a tone, not merely to our village life, but to the concept of life with which we grew up. They seemed to speak for a certainty, for an assured viewpoint, for a standard of values which did not fluctuate, that put such things as bravery, patriotism, confidence in the progress of the human race, and the belief in a broadening freedom for all men, at the very basis of what men moved by.

77

The typical "between wars" books (and, in the past seventy years, movies) about war did the same thing. Most of these—particularly those slanted toward children or adolescents—extol the same qualities. Without fear and without reproach, they exemplified great virtues and gave us role models. The few books and movies showing the other side of war, such as *All Quiet On the Western Front* and *Journey's End*, were far less numerous, less widely noticed (particularly among the adolescent and preadolescent groups), and much less mythic in nature.

There were no popular pulp magazines called *Peace Stories* or *Peace Makers*, but a great many *War Stories*, *Air-War Stories*, and the like. And while some of the fiction in such literary magazines as *The New Yorker*, *Story*, or *Harper's* may have shown the horrors of war, none of the far more widely read pulp magazines did so. They showed instead war's heroic, mythic, and patriotic aspects. They stood for "honor and faith and a sure intent," for courage, belief in the future, and a faith in the best ideals of one's country. These stories, novels, and movies often did not praise war directly, but they did praise the warrior—think of movies like *Sergeant York*, or the vastly popular Horatio Hornblower novels, or numerous other war films. The lesson of this entire genre is that war gives greater meaning, intensity, and purpose to life: it makes one more vital, important, and *alive*.

J. Glenn Gray, a Fulbright scholar and four-year veteran of combat, returned to France fifteen years after World War II and visited a woman he had worked with in the Resistance:

> . . . living in her comfortable home with her husband and son [she] confessed earnestly: "My life is so unutterably boring nowadays. . . . Anything is better than to have nothing happen day after day. You know I do not love war or want it to return. But at least it made me feel alive as I have not felt alive before or since.

This need for color and meaning in life is a strong and powerful drive. When, because of the atomic bomb, war could no longer promise to satisfy this need (as no human beings are likely to survive the next major war), there was bound to be a search for another way to find this greater meaning, purpose, color, and vitality. Since our culture did not provide an acceptable way, it was perhaps one inevitable result of this search that we would have the greatest drug epidemic in history. Cocaine and heroin are not a very good substitute for war, but they are the best many people have been able to find.

As in so many areas, Freud foreshadowed this concern long ago. (If it is true, as is so often remarked, that all philosophy is a series of footnotes to Plato, it is also true that all psychology is a series of footnotes to Freud.) In his *Civilization and Its Discontents*, he writes:

> Life as we find it is too hard for us; it entails too much pain, too many disappointments, impossible tasks. We cannot do without palliative remedies. . . . We cannot dispense with auxiliary constructions as Theodor Fontane said. There are perhaps three of these means: powerful diversions of interest, which lead us to care little about our misery; substitutive gratifications which lessen it; and intoxicating substances, which make us insensitive to it. Something of this kind is indispensable.

The mythical promises of war have always been a "powerful diversion of interest," to say the least. War also gave us Freud's substitutive gratifications of meaning, value, and intensity in our lives and actions. When these were taken away with the advent of the atomic bomb, which makes war meaningless, removes all possibility of glory, and makes a mockery of "ever after," then a new palliative remedy becomes necessary. All we have left is the third of Freud's three "auxiliary constructions."

There are, of course, many other ways to achieve what war promises besides the use of drugs. For some, participation in an art form will do this. Picasso once said: "Painting is like fighting a bull. Art is life or death." The piano virtuoso Byron Janis told me: "Working at a piano is true self-actualization. Playing in a concert is becoming a 'we.'" Working in the Peace Corps, or ecological organizations such as Greenpeace, or in other social action groups, have been wonderful ways for many to meet these needs. Unfortunately, in this as in all previous generations, only a small percentage of the population have pursued these or similar paths.

As a new generation grew up and found that war had lost its mythic quality, it expressed this new realization in its literature. Typical is the statement made by Jimmy Porter in John Osborne's 1956 play *Look Back In Anger*:

> I suppose people of our generation won't be able to die for good causes any longer. We had all that done for us, in the thirties and the forties when we were still kids. There aren't any good, brave causes left. If the Big Bang does come, and we all get killed off, it won't be in aid of the old-fashioned grand design. It'll just be for the brave, new nothing-very-much-I-thank-you. About as pointless and unglorious as stepping in front of a bus . . .

This is not the place to explore this connection in detail; such study calls for the precise analysis to which the tools of modern sociology and psychology are so well adapted. Nevertheless, if we examine the reasons why war is so attractive to human beings, as well as the reasons why drugs are so attractive, we can see that there are many similarities. The fact that the perceived mythic nature of war diminished so much after the atomic bomb (and after the TV coverage of the U.S.-Vietnam carnage), and that shortly thereafter the greatest drug epidemic in history appeared, is surely no coincidence. Furthermore, we are not going to solve the drug problem by directly opposing it any more than the problem of war was solved by the direct opposition of the League of Nations. We must understand the psychological causes and *attractions* of both in order to decrease their prevalence.

The lack of intensity, meaning, and color in life, the gray life without purpose, is a powerful and painful stimulus to do something—anything—to change it. In *The Age of Reason*, written in the late 1930s, Jean-Paul Sartre shows his characters living lives with no central purpose or meaning. They are for the most part comfortably well off, but there is no zest or enthusiasm. One says, "I have led a toothless life. I have never bitten into anything." In his poem "Gerontion," T. S. Eliot pictures an old man at end of his life. He did not fight "at the hot gates," has not done anything of meaning in his life, has never acted strongly in a critical situation. His life as he looks back on it is empty, useless, and dry. In a more modern vein, the protagonist in novelist Stephen Dobyns' recent *Toting It Up* looks back and discovers that his life has been merely a "twelve-car life," a "two-wife life," a "four-kids life," and so on.

All through *War and Peace*, we see battle raising the characters' levels of thought and feeling, bringing them to spiritual and metaphysical explorations of great intensity. Often during combat individual soldiers exist and live on a much more intense and deep level. Their sense of their own existence and its meaning is far more strong. Men who were mediocrities and nonentities all their lives, like Captain Tushin, can function at levels of heroic high intensity during battle.

In Stendhal's *The Charterhouse of Parma*, the people of Milan have had a long period of living in peace without an army, being protected "for a price by the Austrians." To Stendhal "they had been living in a state of boredom." Then Napoleon arrives: "People saw that to be really happy . . . it was necessary to love one's country with real love and to seek out heroic actions."

Sartre's next book after *The Age of Reason*, called *The Reprieve*, employs the same characters—but now everything has changed for them because they believe that war is coming. No longer do they question their lives, or ask why they are not dead of boredom. On seeing his mobilization notice, one says "That's it! I am about to become interesting."

The amount of direct and vicarious risk taking in which people indulge to make their lives more intense is staggering. Not only do they flock to automobile races, which become more popular the more accidents there are (and research has shown that people's driving behavior is far more reckless leaving the parking lots after races than it is when arriving), but they also engage in active risk taking themselves. For little or no material gain, people climb difficult and dangerous mountains, jump from airplanes with delayed-opening parachutes, stand up on the backs of galloping horses, skin-dive in shark-infested waters, and jump off cliffs into water surrounded by rocky shoals. They race snowmobiles recklessly, ski down dangerous mountain paths, and in an enormous number of other ways risk life and limb for "thrills." Tens of thousands of people regularly go hang-gliding; one hang-gliding enthusiast told me, "It scares the living daylights out of me and everything else seems boring ... " According to CNN, 250 new bungee-jumping centers opened in the United States and Canada in the first half of 1992, and over a million people are expected to use them annually. The popularity of horror movies today is too well known to bother discussing here. As the mythological character of war has declined, the popularity of these other diversions—like the use of hard drugs—has increased.

Roller coasters are also becoming more and more popular, and new and faster ones are being built all over the country at a rate unprecedented in the past. The American Coasters Enthusiasts has tripled its membership in the past five years. Its president explains, "It's the ultimate daring adventure that pushes the edge of our own bravery." The new coasters are far more thrilling than the old ones and feel far more frightening. However, the editor of *Roller Coaster* magazine recently said: "If people really knew how safe they are, roller coasters would lose a lot of their thrill." In this as in other forms of risk taking, one expects to survive. In war, one also expects to be one of the survivors. But the excitement in our feeling of being endangered and close to the precipice sharpens our senses, heightens our feeling of individuality, and makes us feel *alive*.

Another aspect of the perceived meaninglessness that many people feel in their lives is the sense that nothing is really going to change in the future. Things, we feel, will continue pretty much the same as they are now. Then war threatens. As we become more emotionally involved, life becomes more exciting, intense, satisfying. As in a fairy tale, we expect to win because we embody the forces of good, and then when we do win things will indeed be different. All the problems of our life are now one problem, all our troubles are due to one cause, and everything will be better when we win. The world will be different and wonderful when "Johnny comes marching home again," and when we have traversed that "long, long trail awinding into the land of my dreams." Every modern war that took on this mythical quality engendered songs ending with the theme "to the time when I'll be going down that long long trail with you." And the implication was always that at the end of that trail, we would live happily, and meaningfully, ever after. Meaning is returned to our lives in war not only because we are enrolled in a great cause worth dying for (but which we will survive), but also because after the war the meaningfulness, the excitement of being alive, the sharpness of the senses and the vitality of being important and "interesting" to ourselves, will remain forever.

Philip Caputo, in his memoir *A Rumor of War*, described reading some Marine recruiting literature in college:

> ... I had one of those rare flashes of insight: the heroic experience I sought was war; war, the ordinary man's most convenient way of escaping from the ordinary.

The Need For a Greater Sense of Belonging to a Group

> The continuous disasters in man's history are mainly due to his excessive capacity and urge to become identified with a tribe, nation, church or cause, and to espouse its credo uncritically and enthusiastically, even if its tenets are contrary to reason, devoid of self-interest and detrimental to the claims of self-preservation. ...
>
> No historian would deny that the part played by crimes committed for personal motives is very small compared to the vast populations slaughtered in unselfish loyalty to a jealous God, king, country or political system ... the ravages caused by individual self-assertion are quantitatively negligible compared to the number slain out of a self-transcending devotion to a flag, a leader, a religious faith or political conviction. Man has always been prepared to die for good, bad, or completely harebrained causes.
>
> Arthur Koestler

This, I believe, is the answer to the question of whether individual violence (murder for passion or profit, rape, and so on) and war are part of the same psychological spectrum and express the same drives and needs. It is my view that they are not. Individual violence is most typically an expression of self-assertive or self-protective drives; war is most typically an assertion of self-transcending drives.

Certainly inner neurotic or psychotic angers and tensions can be expressed in wartime (as they can in peacetime). The opportunities may be there for such expression in combat, or in vicarious participation in combat, or in hating a socially approved enemy. But our tremendous drive toward war—the very widespread attractiveness of it—is much greater than can be accounted for by these individual drives alone. War attracts us more because of our needs to be closer to others than it does for our needs to express hostility.

J. Glenn Gray writes of his extensive combat experience in World War II:

> Many veterans who are honest with themselves will admit, I believe, that the experiences of communal effort in battle even under the altered conditions of modern war have been a high point in their lives . . . which they would not want to have missed.

> For anyone who has not experienced it himself, the feeling is hard to comprehend, and, for the participants, hard to explain to anyone else . . .

> . . . I am accepted not because of any individual merit on my part, but because I am a fellow in the ranks. I can trust my fellow soldiers . . . because of the role given to me . . . and the limits of the role give me a species of freedom.

Another veteran recalled that he became "one percent of a thing called Company Q."

Philip Caputo wrote in *A Rumor of War* of his long experience in Vietnam:

> I have . . . attempted to describe the intimacy of life in infantry battalions, where the communion between men is as profound

as any between lovers. Actually it is more so . . . devotion, simple and selfless, the sentiment of belonging to each other . . .

And by the third week [of Marine Basic Training] we had learned to obey orders instantly and in unison without thinking. Each platoon had been transformed from a group of individuals to one thing: a machine of which we were merely parts.

"We were closer to each other than we were to our wives." "We all loved each other." "There would never be a question of leaving anyone behind. We all got out or none." These are typical of the comments made by members of one of the most dangerous and high risk units that fought in Vietnam—the Long Range Penetration Unit—at a reunion fifteen years later.

The definitive study of the American infantryman in World War II, *The American Soldier*, again and again makes the point that "belongingness" was the most crucial factor in motivating the soldier to fight. Not individual "ideals," but the desire not to let others in the unit down was what kept them going: ". . . good combat morale which we equate here with good primary group relations." This mirrors Napoleon's explanation of why he lost at Waterloo: "My soldiers had not eaten soup together long enough."

Whether in or out of the combat zone, war creates a sense of belonging in citizens. Together we *share* beliefs, dedication, willingness to sacrifice, a common definition of the evil in the world, and hope for the future. This is stronger, more dependable, and far more meaningful than the pale imitation that occurs when we bond ourselves together in groups as "fans" of this or that baseball, soccer, or football team. When at war, the whole country—or at least its accepting citizens—is at one, with the same interests and goals. No one who shares these is left out. Unless they are extremely strong, our normal human feelings of alienation and loneliness can be laid aside.

Julian Symons writes on the period of the bombing of London:

A wretched time people say. I recall it as one of the happiest periods of my life. Living became a matter of the next meal,

85

the next drink. The way people behaved to each other relaxed strangely. Barriers of class and circumstance relaxed. . . . For a few months we lived in the possibility of a new kind of history. It only just needs saying that the successive pieces of "bad news" which disturbed many people as expressing the consolidation of Nazi power throughout Europe, were to me only the expected proof of an old order breaking up. . . . The sense of two "real" worlds, openly repressive and egalitarian, struggling with each other, was exhilarating. The division of society into opposing forces seemed to be as real as the peace of 1945, when it came, was to appear an illusion.

This brings us to an important problem, but a problem to which, curiously, the social sciences have devoted very little attention. Human beings identify themselves with many different groups of many different sizes; but what conditions influence the preferred (or acceptable) sizes? Why, for example, do soldiers in combat primarily identify with a squad or aircrew instead of the "Nineteenth Corps" or the "Fifth Army"? Why do people generally make such choices as "Jordan," but not "Arab League"; "France," but not "United Nations"; "Kurd," but not "Turk"; "Vermont," but not "New England"; "the Mets," but not "the National League"? Why do people enlist in a war out of an identification with a country, symbolized by such slogans as "Remember the *Maine*" or ". . . the Alamo" or ". . . Pearl Harbor," or a larger cause such as "to make the world safe for democracy," but when fighting in combat identify with much smaller units? During their military training soldiers identify with a company or battalion or, in the case of special elite forces, with that elite organization (Marines, *Falschirmjager*, Airborne, and so forth). In combat the elite forces may sometimes retain that larger identification, but otherwise soldiers begin to identify with even smaller units, of a dozen or less.

This problem is complex. Some people identify themselves with a profession, as we see in the international medical teams that go to disaster areas. Some dedicate their lives to some other international cause—for example, some of the devout Marxists. Some identify primarily with a small-city athletic team or a local high school team, where they know the players personally or at close second hand and often see them in action. Others identify with national teams that they may or may not ever see compete in person.

People become so deeply involved with these identifications that they fight, sacrifice, and die for them. The conflict between fans of the Blue and of the Green chariot teams nearly destroyed the Byzantine Empire in the eighth century. Identification with "the Fatherland" or "the Motherland," and fighting strongly because of further identification with smaller units, have repeatedly devastated Europe in this century and past ones.

Human beings seem to be on a constant search for the "correct," the preferred, size unit with which to identify themselves. Their preference seems to shift under varying conditions, but we have no real idea what these conditions are. One is reminded of a compass needle shifting back and forth as conditions change—i.e., new masses of iron being introduced into its immediate area—and finally settling into a new definition of magnetic north. An assumption might be made that nationalism is such a powerful force because a nation is of a conceptual size that "fits" the needs of most individuals in peacetime, and during those transitional times moving from peace to war. Perhaps we will find that we are able to identify with an international group only under special conditions. So far, as the repeated failures of internationalist movements have shown, these conditions are generally lacking when we need them the most. We desperately need to know what conditions make it possible to *increase* the size of our primary group identifications.

Solving this problem appears to be critical for successful work toward lasting peace. Without new thought in this area we will continue to work blindly. It is certainly amenable to study with the tools available to the social sciences. The first psychologist or sociologist to do a Ph.D. thesis in this field will certainly make a considerable advance in our ability to work for peace, and also make a name for him or herself in the profession.

* * *

As human beings we have fundamental needs both for a strong sense of our own individuality and sharp vividness of experience, and also for the knowledge that we are an integral and accepted part of a group, of something larger than ourselves. Outside of the esoteric spiritual-development schools, limited to only a comparatively few followers because of the long, hard discipline they demand, only war promises to fulfill both needs at the same time. Its danger will sharpen our senses and increase our vitality and our sense of being truly alive. With its offer to include us in a band of brothers, all of whom agree on the source of evil in the world and all of whom are dedicated to the proposition that it must be destroyed, our loneliness, our feelings of alienation, our *anomie*, are eased. The more enthusiastic we become about this, the more we are included in the experience, and the greater and more mythical becomes the cause upon which we are embarked. When war is such an "us-them" situation, everyone can be welcomed into the "us." This eases our pain and stress at profound human levels. The statistics show, for example, that the mortality rate for many diseases, including cancer, goes down when a country is actively engaged in war.

Freud, in his comments on war, wrote:

> The individual who is not himself a combatant—and so involved in the gigantic machinery of war—feels conscious of disorientation and of an inhibition of his powers and activities.

In his excellent description of the behavior of cults in the United States (and of mythic behavior generally in this culture), Arthur Deikman shows that people do not join cults because they are "crazy, but because they have two kinds of wishes. They want a meaningful life, to serve God or Humanity, or they want to be taken care of, to feel protected and secure, to find a home." Deikman goes on to show how people satisfy both of these wishes in the mythic orientation of the cult, with its black-white, us-them viewpoints.

War promises equally to fulfill both of the needs that Deikman describes. It promises greater meaning in one's life without requiring one to go outside the mainstream of one's culture. A London newspaper said in 1940:

> Some day there will be written *The London Tales* and it will be one of the great books of the world. It will make young men say, centuries hence: "I would as soon have been living among the Londoners of 1940 as in the Athens of Pericles. It was one of those periods when the threat of death made men truly alive."

This kind of promise has a very great appeal at all levels of society. Depending on the mores of our particular cultural group we may or may not be able to admit this to ourselves or others; but our species consistently acts in ways that indicate we are *attracted* to the idea of war. Mostly this attraction is concealed and denied; occasionally it is open. A book on the British Army before 1914 includes the following passage:

> Did the other [enlisted] ranks [also] pray for war? Certainly their officers thought so, and undoubtedly many, perhaps most, actually did, but we have few personal accounts of life in the ranks. Wolesley said of men in the 2nd Scottish Rifles: "Our whole battalion was composed of young men, full of life and spirit, and impressed with the one idea that the world was especially created for their own pleasures, of which, to most of us, war was the greatest." Ian Hamilton, writing of the day when the Gordon's Battalion in India learned that it was to take part in the first Boer War (1881), said: "War put me very nearly out of my mind with delight. Bar one private from Glasgow who was said to be in love with a Nautch girl, every single living soul was excited and happy."

Another attractive aspect of war lies in our definition of what makes a superior human being. Samuel Johnson wrote, "Every man thinks meanly of himself for not having been a soldier." There is a larger grain of truth in this than we usually care to admit. Every politician knows that military service, particularly combat service, is worth many votes.

To feel strong and superior is to put the general above the specific, the needs of the group above the self, the goal above the dangers and difficulties on the path to attaining it. These are the central meanings of the terms "bravery" and "courage."

They include steadfastness in moving toward a worthwhile goal—a goal that concerns more than the self and the individual's appetites. It is "For God, for England, for St. George," for "La Gloire," "For The Fatherland," for concern with others in one's squad or company, for a just and good cause, for the good opinion of others, for the worth of the world: it is for these causes that one goes in harm's way.

These matters are generally not much thought of during times of action and danger. It is for the historians and playwrights and novelists and psychologists to try to comprehend later why people behaved heroically. Men under fire or headed for the front have their minds on matters far removed from "why" and much closer to "how." But the irrationality of combat demands explanation if we are ever to be able to prevent the Ragnarok and ensuing Fimbul Winter that surely will follow the next atomic conflict. You cannot stop a major and dangerous symptom for very long without an understanding of its causes.

* * *

For a long time there has been a general belief that war was much more attractive to men that it was to women. This belief was a major force behind the fight to give women the vote—the belief that they would vote for peace candidates and issues and make war at least less frequent. People often wrote of war as if only men were involved; Paul Fussell, who knows a great deal about war, writes "Until we redefine manhood, we shall not end war."

There is, however, no real evidence that women are less attracted to war than are men. Giving women the vote has had no noticeable effect on the frequency or ferocity of wars. It has become increasingly plain that the reason women have been less involved in war than men is only that they have not been offered the opportunity to participate more fully. As opportunities have been made for women to join the armed forces or to engage in combat, there have been plenty of volunteers to fill the new positions and even demands by women for more opportunities, including combat service. The attraction to war is a human characteristic, apparently not limited by gender.

Margaret Mead described some of the typical questions asked her by American young people in 1942:

> The girls ask: "How is a girl to nourish the love of war in her boyfriend who seems curiously reluctant to enlist, and should she?"

Women as well as men follow the bugle. Not only has the women's vote failed to produce any greater peace in the nations where it was available, but there has never been a hint of any *Lysistrata* program (a women's sexual or other strike until peace was declared) put into action. By and large, women seem to have been too busy cheering on the troops to have seriously contemplated any specifically "female" protest.

Perhaps because they were denied actual decision-making power in the arena of war, as well as any opportunity to engage in combat, some women have proved to be even more blood-thirsty than men. J. Glenn Gray reports:

> Many a combat soldier in World War II was appalled to receive letters from his girl friend or wife, safe at home, demanding to know how many of the enemy he had personally accounted for and often requesting the death of several more as a personal favor to her.

Every colonial army was warned about the danger of being captured and turned over to the women for torture. In Kipling's advice to the young British soldier in India, we find:

> If you're wounded and left on Afghanistan's plains
> And the women come out to cut up what remains,
> Just roll to your rifle and blow out your brains,
> And go to your death like a soldier.

* * *

There was one way in which the Persian Gulf War was a complete success, although it is impossible to say if this was a conscious goal in the minds of U.S. government or Pentagon officials. The Gulf War once again made war *acceptable* to a very large part of the U.S. population.

The Vietnam War had done the opposite. The grinding, terrible jungle fighting; the television and other graphic media coverage showing the lack of glory and the death and ghastly suffering of so many people, military and civilian alike; the sensory quality of the Americans' perception of the conflict as having no clear goals; all worked to turn that war from the possibility of a heroic crusade into nothing more than jungle killing and more killing. It was a war that, for most American citizens, clearly would make no major difference in the long run. It was, therefore, perceived simply as murder and destruction. The television coverage revealed the truth of what was going on, even in the face of constant Pentagon reports of successes and victories.

As the war went on, even those who had seen a mythical quality in it at first tended to lose that view in the face of contrary, visually presented information. Most of those who had believed in the value of the war changed over the course of time from seeing the war in heroic terms to seeing it in terms typified by the My Lai massacre. It became a sensory war, and therefore unacceptable to a large majority of Americans. The protest marches (try to imagine one of those during World War I or II), the anger at the returning veterans (there were few yellow ribbons, and no ticker tape parades), the rejection of President Johnson, all testify to this shift from the mythical to the sensory. Not only the Vietnam War in particular, but war in general became unacceptable to a large percentage of the U.S. population.

The U.S. attacks on Grenada and Panama were too swift and essentially meaningless to have much effect on American public opinion about war. There was no psychological preparation; they were over before most people had really accepted the fact that they had begun. To most they seemed more like military training exercises than anything else. Their effect on the U.S. population was very small; if anything they increased the public's negative view of war. For the U.S., with its tremendous arsenal and its highly touted armed forces, attacking Grenada seemed more like bullying than war. And again, as during the Vietnam War, the media kept raising questions and pointing out the errors and weaknesses of the military activity: the failure to trap Noriega, the accidental bombing of a mental hospital in Grenada, and so on.

The Persian Gulf War, however, changed all that. We had an enemy with "the fourth largest army in the world." We were repeatedly told of their battle experience, of the elite "Republican Guard," of its modern tanks and artillery, of its skill at defensive warfare. The media as a whole was magnificently managed by the military, showing how well the military had learned the lessons of the Vietnam fiasco. There was a mythic goal—a "New World Order" in which the forces of aggression would be stopped by the civilized forces of the world, led by the United Nations.

The buildup (and psychological preparation) of "Operation Desert Shield" went on for months. No one was killed, and the U.S. population saw constant pictures of our armed forces arriving in Saudi Arabia and preparing for battle. Brave allies were on the scene and the media was careful to avoid all criticism of them. (For example, we all conveniently forgot Syria's coddling and protection of international terrorist groups.) All our problems became one problem as the usual murders, rapes, and violence in the streets vanished from the television news programs. The war was now a fully mythic one.

Then the bombing began. We had fascinating television pictures of "smart bombs" finding their way down the chimneys of Iraqi fortresses and strong points, but no pictures—or even hints that they existed—of the human beings inside. There was a lightning victory—all over machines and artillery. Again, no dead persons appeared to exist. Our targets were only fortified positions and machines, and there were pictures of mile after mile of destroyed Iraqi vehicles—all apparently empty.

And then—at the war's peak—we stopped. On our side, at least, no one except for a few "heroes" had been killed, and these were brought home with flag-draped coffins and solemn ceremonies. War had indeed been changed. Months after the fighting ended, cities were competing to have the best and biggest victory parades, and our returning soldiers were all heroes. It was a wonderful war in every way. Never mind that the Persian Gulf is now an ecological disaster of the first magnitude; that Saddam Hussein is as firmly in power as he ever was; that the Kuwaiti emirs we returned to power are clearly despicable feudal barons; that the groups we encouraged to rise up against Saddam died by the thousands; and other small facts of this kind.

Not only was the Persian Gulf War different from the Vietnam War, it was the cleanest, most bloodless, most ideal picture of war we had seen since before war correspondents first began reporting during the Crimean War. The military had at last, after a century and a half, solved the dilemma of how to present war to the civilian population. For much of the U.S. population, war is once more an acceptable way to solve problems.

The meaning of this change for our future is still unclear. So far, the new acceptability of war does not apply to nuclear warfare. But we have—in the United States at any rate—entered a new era. Whether this was a conscious goal of the U.S. government and our military officials is, as I mentioned before, impossible to know at this time. But planned or not, the effect is clear.

* * *

In this chapter we have illustrated some basic aspects of what attracts the individual to war. War offers us a wonderful target for the tensions and angers we feel toward others who are close to us. These tensions usually make life and adjustment difficult—ambivalence is hard for most people to bear, as is anger at individuals with whom we must maintain a relationship, such as colleagues and superiors at work. When we are offered a way of channeling these tensions to people far away, and we are socially encouraged to use it, our close relationships then improve rapidly and strongly.

War also helps to ease the stresses within ourselves. What is most disliked and rejected about the perceived self—what gives us the most pain or anxiety or depression—can now be projected far away from us, again with full social approval. The energy behind our self-doubts and self-criticisms is now directed outward rather than inward. Our emotional life becomes far simpler.

An evil enemy also solves one of the great human conflicts: how to solve the two drives toward, on the one hand, making one's own life more intense, *felt*, and meaningful, and on the other hand, becoming more of an accepted and integrated member of a group. Usually these are believed to be antithetical; we can either individualize or socialize ourselves. But we know we need to satisfy both drives, as we need both food and water, in order to survive.

The intensity of feeling in war—the danger, the excitement, the implied (and accepted) promise that everything will be vastly better after victory, the engagement in a great crusade for a noble cause—all make our life more exciting and meaningful. At the same time, as crusaders we are very much a part of a group; the more enthusiastic we are, the more dedicated and involved, the more we are accepted into that group. Here is a solution to the great problem—the more we intensify our lives and make them more exciting, the more we find ourselves belonging and accepted. *Not* to be involved and enthusiastic means expulsion from our social groups; we become isolated outsiders.

These psychological pressures in favor of accepting the proposed enemy as a real enemy, to be fought with all our strength, are very powerful. Only war offers the full satisfaction of all four of the motivations discussed here. Seen in these terms, the wonder is not that there are so many wars, but that there have not been more.

Let us make no mistake. War not only promises these satisfactions, but also often delivers them, if only on a temporary basis. (The promise of a permanent solution is ignored after peace comes.) It is unfashionable today to say anything positive about war, but the record indicates that its promises are not always lies.

On March 24, 1991, less than a month after the Persian Gulf

95

fighting had ended, a front-page report in the *New York Times* said the following:

> When the war with Iraq ended on February 28, many Americans sighed with relief, and many smiled with pride. For a precious few days, the euphoria stilled domestic disputes and indulged a national daydream about solving economic and social woes with something akin to six weeks of surgical bombing. Then America woke up, and the recession was still playing on the clock radio.
>
> In interviews last week, sociologists, economists and poll takers, not to mention plastic surgeons, letter carriers and surfboard salesmen, spoke of a perplexing period of rising and falling moods and expectations.
>
> "What Americans are telling me," said Samuel W. Kaplan, a professor of sociology at Swarthmore College, "reminds me of what Rita Hayworth once said about herself: 'Men go to bed with Rita Hayworth and wake up and find it's only me.' America went to bed with a great victory and woke up with a victory that no longer seems so great and a world filled with problems that we basically aren't able to do anything about."

In the winter of 1863–1864, the term of service for most Union Army soldiers (at that time, three years) had run out. These were the experienced soldiers the army needed, but their enlistments had expired. Historian Bruce Catton describes the situation:

> There was no way on earth the government could compel them to stay in the army if they didn't want to. The government had already given these soldiers an object lesson about the folly of volunteering through its abominable conscription act. [Men were drafted unless they had the money to hire a substitute or to pay a special fee.] Then it suddenly had to go to these men hat in hand, and ask them to reenlist.
>
> It's amazing, but many of them did stay on. These were men who had been through the mill. They had been through the terrible battles, Shiloh, Chancellorsville, Gettysburg and Chickamauga. They had survived them, knew what it was like, and knew that even worse fights were coming. They had done their duty and were entitled to go home. In spite of all this, many of them voluntarily reenlisted ... in the Army of the Potomac close to 30,000 volunteers reenlisted that winter of 1863–64, a larger number did so in the West ... [Further] A

great many of the veterans whose time had expired in the Spring of 1864 and who went home to enjoy life as civilians, began by the end of the year to drift back into the army. Some of the regiments that were formed at the end of 1864 and the beginning of 1865 were first-rate regiments because they were full of veteran soldiers . . . who knew their way around in the army and had come back . . .

William Manchester had been safe in a hospital with a wound during the Okinawa campaign in World War II. Hearing that his marine company was going on a dangerous mission, he left the hospital without permission and rejoined them. In the mission he was severely wounded. Many years later he returned as a civilian to the place where he was wounded:

And then in one of these great thundering jolts in which a man's real motives are revealed to him in an electrifying vision, I understand at last, why I jumped hospital that Sunday thirty-five years ago and, in violation of orders, returned to the front and almost certain death.

It was an act of love. Those men on the line were my family, my home. They were closer than any friends ever had been or ever would be. They had never let me down and I couldn't do it to them. I had to be with them, rather than let them die and me live with the knowledge that I might have saved them. Men, I now know, do not fight for flag or country, for the Marine Corps or glory or any other abstraction. They fight for one another. Any man in combat who lacks comrades who will die for him, or for whom he is willing to die, is not a man at all. He is truly damned.

Although Manchester's insight may have been unusual, his behavior was not. For a typical example, let us take a war far removed from the World War II Pacific theatre of operations:

In July 1897, when the 1st Battalion of the Highland Light Infantry was to entrain for the North-West Frontier to fight in the Malakand campaign, invalids left their beds and boarded the train. When the adjutant discovered them he placed them all under arrest, but soon relented and let them come.

* * *

97

Only war offers a solution to so many needs for so many people. That this is still true today need not leave us pessimistic; there are still ways we can solve the problem of war. In his classic essay "The Moral Equivalent of War," William James made an early and primitive step in this direction. Today we have the knowledge and techniques to go much further.

SIX

War and Governmental Behavior: The Form-Function Hypothesis

> We know more about war than we do about peace—
> more about killing than we do about living.
>
> General Omar Bradley

VERY OFTEN a particular war is clearly to no one's advantage. Nothing is to be gained and much may be lost; and yet it is joined. I am not writing here of those cases where individuals in power clearly want a war (or the surrender of other countries without armed conflict, as did Hitler in Austria, Czechoslovakia, and Poland). It takes the leaders of the government of only one country to start a war: the target government's leaders must either fight or surrender. In many other conflicts, however, the governments of two nations appear to blunder into the war as if they were drunken automobile drivers approaching each other at night, neither in much control of their machines and both weaving back and forth across the road until a collision occurs. We might cite as examples the Crimean War, World War I, and the U.S. incursion into Vietnam.

Before the Crimean War was declared, the British prime minister and the London *Times* were against it. Queen Victoria and Prince Albert were undecided.

> On March 27 . . . war was declared. The precise causes and object of the war remained obscure. It was puzzling to find the British nation fighting on the side of Mohammedans against Christians even if Palmerston was right when he said that had nothing to do with the question. Mr. Disraeli's explanation did not seem much more satisfactory. He remarked that he thought we were going to war to prevent the Emperor of all

the Russias from protecting the Christian subjects of the Sultan of Turkey. And John Bright told the House of Commons that he could see no adequate reason for the conflict. . . . After it was over Lord Stanmore said sadly that it had been undertaken to resist an attack that was never threatened and probably never contemplated.

The start of World War I is also a classic example of the erratic and confused leadership that marks the period preceding many wars. Its course, however, is too well known to bear repetition here. Less well known, perhaps, is the course leading to the German government's decision to wage unrestricted U-boat warfare in 1916, a decision that brought America into the war and insured Germany's defeat. This decision was opposed by the chancellor, the vice-chancellor, the foreign office, the German ambassador to the United States, most leading bankers, and the Social Democrats in the Reichstag. The kaiser was assailed by uncertainties, but nevertheless the deadly decision was made. The chancellor's liaison with the navy wrote in his diary for April 24, 1916: "Germany is like a person staggering along an abyss, wishing for nothing more than to throw himself into it."

In her detailed description of the inefficiency and confusion with which governments often stumble into war against their own interests, Barbara Tuchman writes of the Vietnam War:

Ignorance was not a factor in the American endeavor in Vietnam . . . although it was to become an excuse. Ignorance of country and culture there may have been, but not ignorance of the contraindications, even the barriers, to achieving the objectives of American policy. American intervention was not a progress sucked step by step into an unsuspected quagmire. At no time were policy makers unaware of the hazards, obstacles and negative developments. American intelligence was adequate, informed observation flowed steadily from the field to the capital, special investigative missions were repeatedly sent out, independent reportage to balance professional optimism—when it prevailed—was never lacking. The folly consisted not in pursuit of a goal in ignorance of the obstacles but in persistence in the pursuit despite accumulating evidence that the goal was unattainable, and the effect disproportionate to the American interest and eventually damaging to American society, reputation and disposable power in the world.

. . . the Joint Chiefs were thoroughly skeptical. . . . they concluded in an unambiguous memorandum of August 1954 that it was "absolutely essential" to have a "reasonably strong stable civil government in control" and that it was "hopeless to expect a United States training mission to achieve success." They foresaw "a complete military vacuum" if French forces were withdrawn . . . and they judged in conclusion that the United States "should not participate."

Despite this advice and knowledge, the United States did, of course, participate, with the predicted failure and disaster.

* * *

The strangest aspect of this area is the difference in efficiency in the way governments avoid war and the way they wage it. Once it has declared war, a government's efficiency level seems to increase very rapidly. Troops are raised, trained, and dispatched. This is always executed far more efficiently than are any efforts to prevent war.

Generally speaking, governments always operate in a fairly efficient manner in attaining their purposes. Mostly, of course, this purpose is to maintain the overall present power structure and the present reward systems. Governments are also effective in maintaining military systems. (These systems, however, may not be very flexible; they may be better adapted to the last war than the present one. In the past, military technique has changed only very slowly. The phalanx, for instance, was used from Sumerian times in the fourth millennium B.C.. through Macedonian times around 300 B.C. It took hundreds of years before Epamonides invented the uneven battle line that changed Greek battle technique radically. The mass charge was used long after it was outmoded by the invention of accurate rifles, and its use resulted in the death of many thousands as late as 1917. Pickett's Charge at Gettysburg was only one deadly example of this.)

The fact that governments are so inefficient in preventing war (to a degree far greater than in their usual functioning, or in the prosecution of a war once it starts), even in situations where it is clearly against their own interests to fight, is of major importance to our understanding the psychology of war. What has been referred to as "the fog of war," the confusion of the battlefield, actually starts *before* the war is joined.

One place we might look for some understanding of this is in the history of governments. The present system of government grew by small steps. I will put forward here what I shall call "the form-function hypothesis" of governments.

In the ancient world, war was regarded as a natural part of human life. Thucydides quotes the Athenian ambassadors, who justified their aggression by stating, "It has always been a rule that the weak should be subject to the strong." At one time, organized piracy was regarded as an honorable and legitimate profession and "the same system of armed robbery prevailed in the land." A major (perhaps *the* major) function of a government was to protect its citizens from hostile armies and to bring them slaves and goods by raid and conquest. Cleared and arable land, food, and many manufactured goods were most economically obtained by successful warfare and pillage. Certain types of manual labor "belonged properly to slaves" and it was the government's function to obtain them. The natural way to fame and honor was through military adventures, and these were generally seen as "the only act of any importance during a reign" to the degree that military success was considered the natural way to decide the size and placement of statues dedicated to a ruler.

In the view of the universe prevailing in the ancient world, war was an accepted and reasonable way to solve problems (just as the "appeal to arms" was later legally regarded as a reasonable way to attain justice) and the major and legitimate function of government. Therefore, governments were so organized as to be able and ready to use war as a policy. Their form was largely determined by this function.

Our present structure of government is descended from those of the ancient world, modified through centuries of experience and thought during which war was still regarded as the central function of government. (It is not until the seventeenth century that we begin to see the concept of peace discussed as a natural, reasonable, and permanent state.) This long period of development in government shaped its form still further, until the function of effective war-making potential was built into our present forms of government.

The research and thinking available today on the interaction between form and function is far too voluminous and varied to be presented here. This research started almost simultaneously in a large number of fields in the late nineteenth and early twentieth century. In anatomy, for example, we find men such as the Romanian Karel Ranier demonstrating how the needed function shapes the form of a muscle, and how this form later determines what the muscle can and cannot do—its function. In architecture, historians like Krautheimer showed how the Christian liturgy shaped the form of the early churches and how this form later influenced their function. Ever since Louis Sullivan coined the phrase "form follows function" in 1880, architects have gradually learned to insist that the design of a building must start with an analysis of its function. (In 1920, Le Corbusier stated the idea in an uncompromising way in his famous definition of a house as a "machine for living.") A. R. Radcliffe-Brown applied the concept to anthropology and showed that the form of a social system affects the consciousness and behavior (the functioning) of its members. Talcott Parsons demonstrated the importance of the concept in sociology. In linguistics, Alfred Korzybski and others (later including the brilliant Marshall McCluhan) described in detail how the form of a communication system affected the functioning of those using it. In a wide number of other areas of learning, the concept has proven of immense value.

Today we understand that function strongly influences form and form strongly influences function. The structure of a group, a government, or a machine will have a profound, often hidden, effect upon its actions, exerting a constant pressure to move, react, behave in certain ways. In a way, these are tropisms set up by the structural relationships of the parts—built-in tendencies to behave in certain ways.

When conflict between countries begins, governments are inefficient in halting the escalation process precisely because of this form-function relationship. Governments are built on an original design whose major function was to make war, not to maintain or make peace. As an obvious holdover from this past, every government today has officials in charge of "war" or "defense" at its highest level. Nowhere, to my knowledge, is there an official at similar levels in charge of "peace." With our long experience in what a government is and should be, the very idea seems staggering.

The latest edition of the *Encyclopedia Britannica* has a long article on "The Functions of Government." Nowhere is the function of peacemaking mentioned; however, there *is* extensive discussion of the function of making war. (Walter Cronkite, appearing on the CBS Evening News on the second day of the bombing of Iraq by the United States, said "The government has spent five months preparing for the war and has made no preparations for a peace program.")

To take another obvious example: the Constitution of the United States is perfectly clear as to which organ of the government has "the power to declare war." It is nowhere stated which organ has the power to declare peace or to strive to maintain it. These powers have been taken over by the executive branch, which has learned how to negotiate a peace treaty at the end of a war, but has only developed the idea of an active peace program to a minuscule degree compared to the development of active (cold or hot) war programs.

> The grim fact, however, is that we prepare for war like precocious giants and for peace like retarded pygmies.
>
> Lester B. Pearson
> Nobel Peace Prize address, 1957

Henry Adams, looking back on his experience in the inner governmental circles in Washington in 1860, writes:

> Not one man in America wanted the Civil War or expected it or intended it. A small minority wanted secession. The vast majority wanted to go on with their occupations in peace . . . none planned it.

War, then, seems to be a "natural" way of behaving for governments descended from those that evolved during an historical period when war was seen as the central function of government. A constant, deeply concealed pressure *toward war* is theoretically exerted by their structure, a structure "designed" partly for this particular purpose.

Here is an area that modern social science, with its knowledge of and experience with groups and group structure, is admirably suited to explore. If such a pressure does exist, it should be possible to analyze it and develop practical ways of correcting it. At the very least, an analysis of the present system of government must be made as to how its structure (its form) affects its ability to work for peace.

SEVEN

A Beginning

I think it not improbable that man, like the grub that pre-
pares a chamber for the winged thing it has never seen
but is to be—that man may have cosmic destinies that he
does not understand. And so beyond the vision of bat-
tling races and impoverished earth I catch a dreaming
glimpse of peace.

Oliver Wendell Holmes

I AM NOT SO ARROGANT as to believe I can end the
scourge of war with a book. This will take time and all of
humankind working together. There are, however, a few ideas I
have as to how we can work toward that goal, which grow out
of the concepts presented in the previous chapters. They are,
perhaps, a small start.

* * *

On the sixth of August, 1945, the day when the first atomic
bomb was used at Hiroshima, the human race was placed on the
endangered species list. War, an activity practiced by nearly all
human societies as far back as we have records, was suddenly
not only outmoded, but potentially race-suicidal. And make no
mistake: unless there are radical changes in human understanding and behavior, we will use the atomic bomb again. Our track
record shows that we have always used every new technology,
from iron-smelting to radio, for military purposes. We have
never yet given up any weapon available to us as long as it was
effective. Unless we make major changes, we will use nuclear
fission again. The political picture may have changed in the past
few years, but not the mainsprings nor the interaction patterns
of human behavior.

The answer to the question "What would happen if they gave

a war and nobody came?" has always been that a large percentage of the people *do* come. With very few exceptions, no matter what their religion or political orientation or intellectual level or knowledge of history or experience of other cultures, they fight. A. E. Housman wrote despairingly of the terrible side of war, of its uselessness and of "lovely lads and dead and rotten," but sadly concludes that he too would follow the martial call:

> Far away the bugles hollo
> High the screaming fife replies.
> Gay the files of scarlet follow:
> Woman bore me, I will rise.

Despite the many simplistic theories on war that have often gained wide acceptance, wars are waged by human beings raised using every known method of childhood training and in all known forms of society. Whether raised and living in a tribe, a city-state, a farm community, a village, or a metropolis; whether living in a commune, an autocracy, a theocracy, or a republic; whether living in a fascist, a democratic, or a communist state; the tendency to follow the bugles seems about the same. Whether raised and living in a matriarchy or a patriarchy; a society where children are treated primarily with love and warmth, or primarily with harshness and restriction; whether economic conditions are prosperous or not, stable or in flux; whether the actual combat is near to or far from home; none of this appears to make very much difference. It comes down to this: human beings identify themselves with social units that frequently declare war on each other, and that will pick up weapons and try their best to kill each other.

There are a few exceptions; the Quakers, Amish, Eskimo, California Mission Indians, Kalahari Bushmen, and a very limited number of others. No one, to my knowledge, has tried to find out what factors are common in these groups and not in others.

It is easy enough when examining the history of each war to find the exact series of circumstances that led to it: the angers, the fears, the complaints, the clashing interests, the broken treaties. However, as Thucydides warned us long ago, we must look beyond the specific events if we are to understand the real causes of even one war. How much further, then, must we look behind the specific events if we are to understand the problem of war in general? We must not ask, "What events led to the outbreak of this war or that one?", but rather, "What is there in man that makes him so ready to go to war, in almost all cultures or economic conditions?" The question we are dealing with here concerns the readiness, the receptivity, the seed-bed on which specific events fall and which, when nourished by it, flower into armed intergroup conflict.

The basic task set forth is the prevention of wars in general. They are a fact of human behavior: widespread, easily stimulated into being, terribly difficult to prevent or control. "History is a bath of blood," wrote William James. Whether rich or poor, single or married, in rigid or flexible cultures, human beings gather in armies and fight other armies. Arthur Koestler put it aptly: "The most persistent sound which reverberates through man's history is the beating of war drums." Neither religion nor political orientation has had much effect on war. Nor has "progress." In the words of one study of the subject: "The 'information revolution' has done everything but pacify the hearts of men."

Nor have the usually suggested "social" methods of averting war (such as promoting greater interaction among nations) seemed to bear much relationship to the problem. In June 1914, for example, more Europeans were traveling, conferring, holidaying and working in foreign countries than ever before. The Channel steamers and international trains were jammed, there was a babble of languages at German spas and Riviera resorts, a long list of international conferences organized for the summer all over Europe, warehouses of foreign goods in Hamburg, Manchester, Vienna, and St. Petersburg. Business was excellent; international trade was doing very well. During the next two months, the greatest war in human history up to that date got into full swing.

* * *

Our first protection against war will have to be an *awareness* on the part of the public at large that war does serve, and has always served, as a very tempting and attractive way to solve many intrapersonal and interpersonal problems. Further, we are still, in spite of our hopes and our wishes to be different, extremely vulnerable to this temptation. In spite of the fact that war has been a successful way (even with its horrendous price tag) to solve these problems in the past, it does not work any longer. It is most important that we realize *there are other ways to solve these problems and receive the psychological benefits provided by war*.

Part of this process must entail an increase in our awareness that there is a strong tendency in us humans to shift our method of appraising an international situation from a sensory reality to a mythic reality as tensions escalate. This is a switch from a method of organizing reality that can solve problems by reason *or* force to a method that can *only* solve problems by force.

If there is general awareness of this kind of change and what it portends, then its indications can be picked up early and subjected to analysis. We will then be able to *choose* this shift, and if we choose it, do so with full, conscious awareness. It will be seen as a possible alternative, to be chosen publicly if so desired. It is in the hope of bringing about this public consciousness that I have in this book been so deliberately repetitious about characterizing the different aspects of the sensory and mythic methods of constructing reality.

As an immediate example, try to think back to the morning of February 23, 1991. The American ultimatum to Iraq to leave Kuwait or face a ground war was to expire at noon that day. President Bush had just announced that we were fighting "to establish a new world order." The shift from a sensory organization of the situation, with its limited goal to solve *this* problem for *now*, to a mythical organization with its utopian, total, forever-after goal, was in full swing. Up to then the Persian Gulf War had been a mythic war only for the Iraqis. Now it was also becoming one for the United States. The entire U.S. population was "tipping" on this question. A Gallup Poll released that same morning showed that only 22 percent of those polled were in favor of a cease-fire and negotiations. This was down from well over 50 percent a few brief weeks before. More and more, anti-war sentiments were being seen as "unpatriotic."

If there was greater awareness of the dynamics of this shift from the sensory to the mythic, an alertness toward it, a knowledge that it only permits solutions by force, we could *decide* if we wanted to make this shift. The mythic evaluation of reality is certainly the best way to fight a war. But the decision of *whether* to fight a war should be made in the sensory reality, without the contamination of mythical elements.

I am suggesting that it is now critically important for the population at large to understand that we human beings use different methods of organizing reality, and shift back and forth between them without realizing we are doing so; that each mode of organization has different values and solves different kinds of problems; and that while the mythic reality is better for actually fighting a war, the sensory reality is better for deciding whether to fight a war at all. If this information could become part of conventional wisdom, we would be far more likely to make a decision to go to war (or not to) using the organization of reality best suited to that decision.

One aspect of any decision to fight must be the clear recognition, before going to war, of what that war can accomplish. In the sensory reality evaluation, we understand that a war can solve a particular, limited problem. This problem may well make it worthwhile to go to war. The ambitions of a Hitler to enslave the world, or of a Pol Pot, or of a Saddam Hussein, may be so bad for the rest of us that declaring war against them is a reasonable and logical decision. But no war will accomplish mythical reality, forever-after goals. It will not make the world safe for democracy, nor establish a thousand-year Reich, nor organize a new world order, nor fulfill a Manifest Destiny, nor establish the perfect society, nor end war, nor do anything else except solve a particular problem, at a high cost and with unpredictable changes following it. And there *will* be unexpected and unpredictable changes following any war.

It may be too much to say—as some have said—that whatever you go to war for will no longer exist when the war is over. But there will, afterward, be major changes, and most of these changes will be in unexpected directions.

The cost and uncertainty of war may well be worth the candle. Each decision must be made separately, however, and in a sensory reality evaluation. Not only does the tree of liberty need blood to water it from time to time, but so also does the very tree of life. But do not think that any war will solve problems forever. Rome won a major war and solved the problem of Carthage for several hundred years, but where is Rome today? Simon Bolivar may have won a war and ended the repressive and cruel Spanish control of South America; but no one who looks at the present condition or history of South America will see an Eden.

The old conflict where one person says "War never decides anything," and the other person disagrees, is a confusion of sensory and mythic reality goals. Certainly wars *do* decide some things. There is not a Confederate States of America occupying the southern portion of the United States, nor is there likely to be in the near future. Nor are there concentration camps and extermination programs in Europe and America; World War II prevented that situation. However, we do have new and other problems, which will doubtless continue to be the case. We are not "happily-ever-aftering," and in *that* sense war did not decide anything. That promise of the mythical evaluation of war is never kept.

This suggests the reason for the disillusionment that frequently follows a victorious war. We feel that once the job is done and Evil is defeated, everything will be fine forever. Then we find, after the armistice, that there is still a great deal of work to do and a great many problems to solve before the world will become an Eden, or even a Camelot. We feel angry and deceived. Then, as the Great Cause dissolves in our minds, it becomes inconvenient to think of the war wounded and dead as heroes. We begin to see them as dupes, cannon fodder for Big Oil, Wall Street, The King, or what have you. Money for veterans hospitals becomes hard to find in peacetime. If, in a time of economic depression, veterans go to the Capitol to demand financial help, the government has no hesitation in calling out the army to disperse them.

It is clear that the public at large is no longer emotionally involved with yesterday's heroes. They belong to a story of which we no longer feel a part. Their tale (in which we were once so deeply involved) is now "long ago and far away." We have left the mythic evaluation of reality, in which they played so large a part, returning to the sensory evaluation and leaving them behind. The public makes this shift from time to time, back and forth, with no particular difficulty. However, those for whom war provided the greatest meaning in their lives, and those who were wounded, physically or psychologically, are largely left behind: confused, often bitter, frequently deeply disappointed. The professional soldier observes these changes and accepts them, but doesn't like them very much. In Kipling's words, he knows that:

> It's 'Tommy this' and 'Tommy that' and
> 'Tommy go away,'
> But it's 'Thank you Mr. Atkins' when the
> bands begin to play.

* * *

Many wars are blundered into that obviously will accomplish nothing. A shift into a mythical evaluation of the situation, the psychological advantages and promise of a war, the lack of governmental structure to maintain peace—all of these elements combine and suddenly armies are at each other's throats. As examples, there are the Crimean War, the Boer War, World War I, and the Vietnam War. Other wars start with one country taking a mythical view of the situation and other countries being forced to respond with arms or else surrender. Typical here are World War II, the Arab-Israeli wars, and the Italy-Ethiopia War.

The existence of the atom bomb has seriously changed the balance, in sensory reality, of when going to war is a logical activity. The bomb can *never again* be disregarded. Wars can be fought without it (it was not used in the dozens of wars that have occurred since 1945), but it is always a terrible danger.

113

However, in the face of a new Hitler or Stalin, war may still be a logical course of action.

But—this decision *must* be made today with a sensory evaluation that can deal with all the known factors and dangers. And it can *only* be made from this viewpoint if there is common knowledge that there are two (at least) methods of evaluating reality, knowledge of what these methods are, and awareness that both methods are often used in these evaluations.

It is only in the sensory reality that one can learn from experience or from history. In the mythic reality, the rules and the construction of the world are so firmly set that little learning occurs. We follow our *concepts* of "what is," rather than examine and learn from what is happening. This is why, for example, neither we nor the Germans stopped bombing civilian targets even after long experience had shown that such bombing did not interfere much with war production and that it tended to strengthen rather than weaken civilian morale and determination. Even after the experience of World War II and the after-war evaluations of civilian bombing, the United States continued the practice in Vietnam.

As part of promoting this "awareness" in the public at large, it may be advisable here to make a "check list" of specific changes in the ways we think and communicate that indicate we are shifting from a sensory reality evaluation to a mythic reality evaluation. If we are aware of these specific indicators, and watch for them in ourselves, each other, and the media, we will be at least partially inoculated against making the shift unconsciously. We may well decide we want to make the shift *after* we go to war. We certainly should not welcome it before we have made the decision to fight.

Such a check list might be something like the following:

1. We begin to devalue the other side. Attributes begin to be divided: generally speaking, the good ones to us and our "brave allies," the bad ones to them and their "spineless satellites." Further, all members of the enemy group are perceived as similar. Their individual characteristics drop out

114

and only the negative stereotype is left. This is the "Prussian," or "Hun," or "Gook," or "decadent English," or "Dink," or "little yellow bastards" syndrome; it frequently exists side by side with lip service to the idea that "We have no quarrel with the Ruritanian people, only with their leaders."

2. There is a rapid loss of interest in the *reasons* for the differences between "us" and "them." Different is just how we are —we are good and benevolent, they are evil and ambitious.

3. Contrary ideas become dangerous to express. They mark one as a person to be avoided or punished. Expressing opposition to a prevailing orthodoxy becomes hazardous, first to a person's reputation, second to his or her physical safety. In the McCarthy period, very few high schools or colleges invited Communists to address them. The very idea of a public address entitled "The German Point of View" being advertised in 1917-1918 or 1942-1945 strikes us as ludicrous or traitorous. During the Korean and Vietnam wars, how many television panels and discussions do you remember where there was a strong presentation of "the North Korean viewpoint," or "how the North Vietnamese see the war"?

4. Those who even *question* the accepted wisdom are condemned, first as "unpatriotic," later as "traitors," "saboteurs" and so on. They are seen as dangerous and must be dealt with quickly, efficiently, and ruthlessly.

5. Moral standards are no longer applicable to our dealings with "those people," as they would only work to our disadvantage. It was seen as perfectly reasonable in World War II to put Japanese-Americans in "relocation" camps without trial, and to confiscate their homes, farms, and stores. Since all "Japanese" (including second- and third-generation American citizens) were seen as alike—devious, sinister, and ruthless—this procedure was perceived as not only acceptable but necessary.

6. "Our" actions are judged differently than "their" actions. It was legitimate for us to bomb civilian centers in Baghdad. It was not legitimate (and was furthermore proof of their evil

nature) for the Iraqis to send random Scud missiles against civilian centers in Saudi Arabia or Israel. There were similar differences in the moral judgments we and the Germans made during World War II about the aerial destruction of Coventry and Hamburg.

7. The goal of the war shifts from the solution of a present, specific problem (ending the insane ambitions of a Hitler, keeping the United States from fragmenting, forcing the Iraqi soldiers out of Kuwait) to a "glorious cause" (making the world safe for democracy, establishing a new world order) that will solve all our problems. The unspoken belief appears that this is *the* crucial battle between good and evil, and after it is won we will have no more problems. Once we start "happy-ever-aftering," we have shifted to a mythic viewpoint.

One aspect of this shift is a loss of interest in discussing the causes of the war. It becomes more and more the accepted wisdom that the war is simply one more example of the *evil* of the enemy.

There are other possible points to add to this check list. One would be the appearance of a "Teflon factor" in our leaders, whereby we quickly forget their mistakes and believe that anything is true simply because our leaders said or predicted it. Another would be the appearance of the belief that great cosmic forces ("God," "history," "destiny," "morality") are on our side.

However, even this brief list, if widely known, would help. If a copy of this list (or preferably an even better one) were on every high school, college, and church bulletin board, was repeatedly printed in the newspapers as a warning to readers (perhaps under the heading, "The Surgeon General has determined that mythical thinking at this time is hazardous to your health and may cause radiation burns and the death of your children"), we would have at least a partial protection against making this shift at the wrong time.

This comprehension of our habitual and expert use of different organizations of reality is crucial if we wish to lessen the frequency of war in the atomic age. We must understand and accept the fact that war is attractive to us human beings and that we are easily tempted by its implicit promises. William James wrote, "War taxes are the only ones men never hesitate to pay . . . " and it is important that we learn to accept the implications of this eagerness.

This is very hard for most of us to admit—that war is very attractive to human beings. We prefer to explain war as the work of the devil, whether our particular culture offers a devil with hooves and horns, a devil in man's personal or racial history, a devil called "Wall Street" (or "Big Business" or "The King"), or a devil in the organization of society. There must, we feel, be a culprit somewhere, because we could not behave this way of our own free will. The enthusiasm with which we greet the onset of war, however, makes it hard to maintain a picture of ourselves as unwilling dupes or reluctant draftees. In addition, the almost universal existence of war through all of human history, with its thousands of different governmental organizations, cultural systems, and child-rearing practices, shows that these "culprit" explanations are simply not helpful. General Pershing's comment that humans fight wars because "they enjoy it" may be an overstatement, but it contains far more truth than we usually care to admit. Further, there are just enough exceptions—cultures whose members simply do not comprehend the concept of war—to show that "human nature" is no explanation either.

(The phrase, "That's human nature" is one of those statements that makes the speaker believe he has said something meaningful, when all he has done is uttered a series of sounds that satisfy his curiosity and prevent him from exploring the subject further. When it is used as an explanation of some human action, it could almost invariably be used just as convincingly to explain a completely opposite action. Literally, if a person under scrutiny behaves aggressively in a particular situation or if he doesn't, the description, "That's human nature" is just as valid and convincing.)

* * *

Our second level of protection against our tendency to make war will have to be our educational system.

The first task of any species is the raising of its young. This is our primary business, and when a species raises its offspring in a way that does not prepare them for the environment in which they will live, the species dies.

Human beings do not only live in the primarily physical environment in which wild animals live. They live in a social environment as well. We are as affected by the social world as by the physical, and to separate one from the other, as far as human beings are concerned, is not possible. General social knowledge of how to build and raise a rooftree changed the environment we live in, as did the inventions of double-entry bookkeeping, the postal system, and the automobile. Each technological advance has changed our environment. The atomic bomb has changed it so completely that we will need a radically different technique of educating our young if we wish our species to survive.

Many of my suggestions presented here regarding education are not new. To anyone at all familiar with the history of educational theory, my debt to such figures as Johann Pestalozzi, Friedrich Froebel, and John Dewey are obvious.

If we look at the psychological factors that appear to make war so widespread, we can again organize them into four general, overlapping classifications:

1. The need to reduce inner tensions: to reduce intrapersonal stress.
2. The need to increase one's sense of belonging, of one's meaningful relationships: to reduce interpersonal stress.
3. The need to increase one's sense of self and the meaningfulness of one's existence.
4. The need to use other constructions of reality than the sensory reality: in particular, the mythic reality construction.

If we can raise children so that these needs are satisfied using other means than war, if each child is trained in ways to fulfill these needs without armed intergroup conflict, then we shall have made it far more likely that when they give the next war, nobody will come.

The educational system I put forward here is based on five tracks that all children will pursue from the very beginning of their formal educational experience. These tracks must be kept clear and conscious in the minds of all teachers and students working at all educational levels.

1. To accept, value, express, and celebrate oneself as a unique individual.
2. To accept, value, express, and celebrate oneself as a member of one's local community; to contribute to the community and its needs in the way best suited to one's individual personality.
3. To feel at home in other constructions of reality—in particular the mythic and the unitary; to learn one's own special ways of expressing the mythic reality and accepting one's need to do so; to find one's best ways to feel a part of the larger community of all human life, all sentient life, or the cosmos itself.
4. To attain certain basic skills needed to live and prosper in one's society.
5. To learn how to learn; to find the ways in which one as an individual learns best.

These tracks are put forward in this order for good reasons. To accomplish the second and third well and healthily depends (as all modern psychology teaches us) on a healthy development of the first. The fourth and fifth will usually be accomplished in the course of the first three.

Although the concept of these five tracks must be kept clear and conscious in all of our minds, in practice there will be a good deal of overlap. A specific activity may well involve both tracks one and three, for example. I will briefly discuss these tracks one at a time.

*1. To accept, value, express, and celebrate oneself as a unique
individual.*

This track will ask of each student: "What kinds of activity fill
me with enthusiasm, turn me on, do I really enjoy and 'get lost
in' so when I look up from them I feel good and relaxed and
when I am finished I have that 'good tired' feeling? What can I
do to celebrate and use my uniqueness? In what way am I most
like myself (as opposed to being most like others)? What activities 'sing me' as an individual? What kinds of activity make me
the best company for myself? What do I need in the ways of special skills and knowledge to get the most out of these activities?"

Students at each age level will be presented with a wide variety of possible activities and encouraged to pursue one or more
using these criteria. The encouragement of students' individuality will be a very powerful factor in reducing intrapersonal
stresses now and later in their lives. No matter what theoretical
viewpoint one holds concerning the human psyche, recognition
and encouragement of this sort can only be seen as an aid to
mental health.

*2. To accept, value, express, and celebrate oneself as a
member of one's local community.*

The basic questions this track asks are: "What aspects of group
activity can I participate in with most enthusiasm? What expresses and "celebrates" me as a member of the present social
group with which I primarily identify (class, school, community, country)? What activities of the group can I engage in that I
enjoy and which contribute to the group? In what ways am I
most like other members of my group? What can I do to
strengthen the integration of the group and therefore my sense
of belonging to it? What do I need in the way of special skills
and knowledge to do this?"

At each developmental period, and in each general age group,
various activities will be presented—if they do not suggest
themselves—to group members. These will range over as wide a
spectrum as possible, including such possibilities as sports, the-
ater, dance, choral activities, community service, record keep-

ing, finding new ideas and directions for the group, housekeeping, and so on.

3. To feel at home in other constructions of reality.
There are two basic questions addressed on this track. The first is, "What celebrates and expresses me as a member of the human race—what activities can I engage in that will affirm me and also affirm my part in something larger than myself, my immediate family, and my local group—how am I most like all other human beings?" This is the basic approach to the unitary construction of reality. At each age level, appropriate activities will be introduced, ranging from UNICEF fundraising, study of other cultures (different ways of being at home in the world), peace and ecology activities, meditation procedures leading to cosmic consciousness experiences, and so on.

The second question is, "In what other constructions of reality, such as those found in art forms, play, or prayer, can I engage and participate, for no practical value but the sake of my own enjoyment and growth?" Acquiring this sort of knowledge is presented as necessary for the growth and health of the individual, and anyone without the skills to express the mythic construction of reality fully and joyfully (and wishes he or she had more time to devote to this) will be regarded simply as we would a person who has a vitamin deficiency: as someone with a potentially dangerous lack that requires immediate action to deal with it.

4. To attain the basic skills needed to live and prosper in one's society.
An overall list will be made of the skills and knowledge needed to function well in the student's own society. This list will be maintained and updated every so often; skills and knowledge areas would be classified by very general age groupings such as "prepuberty," "late adolescence," or "young adulthood." Most of these skills would be picked up by students in their work on tracks one, two, and three. This list will include such abilities as being able to make change, read, balance a checkbook, listen to and evaluate candidates running for public office, vote with care, look up new information, present one's ideas and point of

view, parent a child, retrieve information from a computer, maintain personal hygiene, drive a car, work cooperatively in a group, work alone, and know some of the great issues of history. If a student has not picked up adequate knowledge in one of these areas at the appropriate age, it will be re-included in the individual curriculum designed—and redesigned from time to time—for this person.

5. To learn how to learn.
As each new activity on tracks one, two, three, and four is experimented with, teachers will help students to attain the knowledge and skills to do it with more zest, completion, and satisfaction. The experience of learning—and of learning how to learn—will be built into the system throughout each program track, helping each student develop as a unique individual, as a member of a local group, and as a participant in the human community, as well as in becoming comfortable with other ways of construing reality.

An education system based on these principles would not turn students into helpless, exploitable pacifists; the first and second tracks would prevent this. Students would know the truth of Archibald MacLeish's statement, "If you turn the other cheek to a Fascist you get your head knocked off." Such a system would, however, develop citizens who had no inner needs to go to war, and to whom war would be acceptable, if necessary, but not tempting.

* * *

A third level of protection against our strong but outmoded tendency to make war on each other lies in the government. The structure of modern governments would be examined for the balance between their ability to make war and their ability to seek and maintain peace. What governmental structures are involved in each process, and what is their relative prestige and power? What changes and additions to governmental structure are needed? Who is in charge of leading the work for peace as the secretary of defense is in charge of leading the work for war? Richard Barnet has noted:

> There are file drawers of contingency plans in the Pentagon for fighting all kinds of wars that can never be fought, but the White House clearly has no contingency plans for what to do in the face of Cold War victory.

Who is making "contingency plans" for peace as the Department of Defense makes for war? This is a question admirably suited to the skills and training of political scientists.

* * *

What I have outlined here is a small beginning. It consists of three areas in which we must work so that the likelihood of future wars can be diminished.

First: we must work toward an increase in public awareness of the fact that war is, for a variety of reasons, a very attractive activity for human beings. War implicitly promises to solve many of the great problems all humans face—how to fulfill at the same time our needs to increase our individuality, ease our internal psychological stresses, increase our sense of belonging to something larger than ourselves, increase the intensity and meaningfulness of our lives, and live in a number of different constructions of reality.

By failing to recognize war's psychological appeal, we make ourselves particularly vulnerable to it. If we are conscious of what is being tempted within us, and are conscious of the signs to watch for indicating that we and others around us are giving in to this temptation, we can increase our control over our behavior.

Second: I suggest a new approach to education, designed to deal with basic human needs so that in the future our new, young citizens will have better ways to fulfill them than we do today. This educational approach is very much in line with what modern psychology tells us children need for their healthiest possible development.

Third: I suggest the need for a study of some special aspects of governmental structure. Such a study would examine the structural reasons for governments' inability to maintain peace with their neighbors. This is an area that has been very little explored by social and political scientists, but the tools for such exploration are now within our grasp. Once the governmental structures pressing toward war, as well as those pressing toward peace, are better understood, new ways of changing government for the better are sure to appear.

* * *

Any serious approach to the problem of war must concentrate on two areas: why war is so attractive to human beings, and why governments so often act against their own interests in moving away from peace. Governments alone cannot fight war; the people must also be involved. In Tolstoy's words:

> If Napoleon had not taken offense at the request that he withdraw beyond the Vistula and not commanded his troops to attack, there would have been no war. But if all the sergeants had been unwilling to serve on another campaign, there could have been no war either.

This must be kept clear if we are to make any progress. Unfortunately, it is a fact often forgotten by theorists of war, who act as if nations are organic entities and only government decisions play any part in the movement toward war. To quote Tolstoy again:

> Napoleon commanded an army to be raised and to march out to war. This conception is so familiar to us, we are so accustomed to the idea, that the question of why six hundred thousand men go out to fight when Napoleon utters certain words seems meaningless to us.

Individuals can kill alone, but they cannot go to war alone. For this they need the large, complex social organization of government. This also is forgotten by certain other theorists, who see only the individual's motivation. Theories of personal aggression (which attribute war either to phylogenetic origin, our "hunting history," or such like causes, or perhaps to childhood experience, as is the view of some psychologists) leave out the problem of government organization. The psychologist Gordon Allport put it:

> Among the attempts to explain national aggression we find two that because of their extreme onesidedness are wrong. One errs in finding all causes to lie in the idiosyncrasies of the individual, the other in finding all causes to lie in the history or the economic imbalance of world society.

It has frequently been pointed out that war has been so common in human history that it is "obviously" a part of "human nature" or "man's greed" or is "inevitable in the socialization process," or what have you—that nothing can be done about it. (These theories are certainly comforting in their ability to lessen both our guilt and our feelings of responsibility over war.) But there is no reason to retreat to an attitude of, "War always has been and always will be. It can't be stopped. Nothing can be done. I told Wilbur and I told Orville and I'm telling you. It can't be done." There have been other social patterns just as widespread as war, and just as widely deemed impossible to dispense with, that we have abandoned. It is only over the last 150 years that we have given up another such practice that had been with humankind since before historical records began. John Dewey wrote in this context:

> War is as much a social pattern as is the domestic slavery that the ancients thought to be an immutable fact.

If we could get rid of slavery, can we not—under the threat of extinction, and using our new knowledge of the social sciences—get rid of war?

The time is now. Every war we have fought and will fight since 1945 increases the chance that someone will again use the atomic bomb, certainly destroying our civilization and in all probability destroying our species. The day the first bomb was dropped was, in Buckminster Fuller's words, "The day that humanity started taking its final exam." We had better pass.

APPENDIX

A Classification System for Self-Destructive Behaviors

History repeats itself, but only in outline and in the large
. . . in a developed and complex civilization individuals
are more differentiated and unique than in a primitive
society, and many situations contain novel circumstances
requiring modifications of instinctive response; custom
recedes, reasoning spreads; the results are less pre-
dictable. There is no certainty that the future will repeat
the past. Every year is an adventure.

Will and Ariel Durant

SINCE AUGUST 6, 1945, it has been clear that the fundamental problem of war has changed. Up to that point, war
always threatened the death of individuals and possibly the
destruction of one or more cultures. It was dangerous for these
reasons, but only for these reasons; in spite of war's horrors, our
species itself was never under assault. The dinosaurs and the
saber-toothed tiger might have gone, and Rome and Carthage,
the Assyrians, the Medes and the Persians, but we human
beings would continue to inhabit the planet no matter how we
hunted and slew each other.

Now this certainty is gone. Any war fought after the light of
the center of the sun blazed over Hiroshima can lead to the possibility of human extinction. If we continue our past pattern, it is
absolutely inevitable that sooner or later there will be a war
between two nations, both of which have atomic weapons.
Then—and this is clear from our human track record—no matter what is promised, no matter what treaties or concordances
have been signed and sworn to, the leaders of the nation that is

losing this war will unleash nuclear weapons. The response is inevitable. Which species, if any, will emerge from the resulting clouds of radioactive dust is impossible to predict, but human— as we know the meaning of the term—it will not be.[1]

Nor can an effective defense against nuclear weapons work for very long. In all our long history of developing offensive and defensive weapons, the balance between the two has repeatedly shifted back and forth. No matter how good a defense is, new developments always give the palm to the offense and then, later, vice versa. Even if we were able to develop the perfect defense of an ideal "star wars" system, developments in new delivery techniques would soon overcome it. If we have not learned the lesson of the Maginot Line (the perfect defense in World War I, completely outmoded by World War II), we are very slow learners indeed.[2]

There is no hope for our species but peace. Period.

Since war has become such an absolutely self-destructive behavior, in spite of which we seem unable to stop, it may well be wise to look at the whole problem of self-destructive behaviors. This appendix is one attempt to do so—to take the psychodynamic experience of individuals acting in self-destructive ways and suggest a new classification system and framework within which to describe them.[3] It is by no means a solution to the problem, but simply an example of the kind of work we need to do. If we approach the problem from a wide variety of viewpoints, we may be able to find a fruitful synthesis for this desperate period in our history.

* * *

In 1909, Stekel introduced the problem of self-destructive behavior into the psychological literature. Spielrein further discussed the matter in 1912, and it was brought to the full attention of the psychological field in 1922 with the publication of Freud's book *Beyond the Pleasure Principle*. This book provoked a great deal of discussion and debate, and an observer at that time would confidently have predicted that much progress in this field would be made in the near future. As we examine the literature after 1922, however, we are surprised to find that our basic understanding of self-destructive behavior has grown very little. This lack of progress is in spite of careful work by scholars of the caliber of Alexander, Federn, Kubie, Menninger, Jelliffe, Symons, and Zilboorg. All of these, and others, have made major contributions to the field, and yet our overall understanding is vague, our concepts cloudy, and our best therapeutic efforts often fail. In view of the tremendous importance of this problem in our era of atomic weapons, our inability to progress toward a solution becomes more challenging than ever.

Our belief that human beings often act in self-destructive ways rests on five classes of information. These are:

Clinical observations of masochism.

Masochistic behavior typically involves hostile and aggressive actions directed at the self. Its incidence is striking and unmistakable. Freud believed that masochism is basic to human beings and sadism is its reversed form.

The well-known fact that people, individually or in groups, often act in ways that inexorably lead to their own self-destruction.

This class would include the depressed suicide, the accident-prone, the polysurgical addict (who manipulates physicians into performing repeated surgical procedures upon him), the alcoholic, and the drug addict. It would also include individuals who believe, in these days of modern weapons, that war is a sane way of settling disagreements. The professional journals, the daily newspapers, and the history books all provide ample testimony to the existence of this class.

The feeling of the psychotherapist, when dealing with certain patients, that they have a deep and tenacious drive toward death.

Such perceptions on the part of experienced therapists are valid data. Frequently their sense of this drive is very strong, and in dealing with a drug addict or a tragedy-prone patient, it may lead the therapist to a feeling of helplessness and defeat before its stubborn and protean characteristics.

The accompaniment of many physical diseases by psychological stress of great intensity, associated at deep personality levels with what appear to be drives to reject life and human relationships.

In labeling these diseases "psychosomatic," we have affirmed our belief that the psychological stress and despair of the patient play a part in their pathogenesis. Today, few would go so far as Groddeck in assessing disease as the direct acting out of unconscious symbolism. However, Rank's concept of the Counterwill gaining ascendance over the Will in disease has influenced our basic thinking about psychosomatic diseases, and the assumption that the patient is organically acting out self-destructive drives is accepted by many.

The fact that statistical studies show that the incidence of self-destructive acts is not random.

Durkheim first pointed out that suicide rates may vary with the rate of change of economic conditions. Marbe and many others since have demonstrated that a person who has had one accident is more likely to have another accident than are those people who are similarly exposed to risk but have had no previous accidents.

The concept of the repetition compulsion is not included in the above list. This is a bold and brilliant construct, but no way has been found to assess its validity. Kubie has shown that this concept is not necessary to explain the data we have. Apparently, it will have to be left as a hypothesis until we can devise a way to test it.

* * *

In general, social scientists have theoretically treated self-destructive behaviors as if they all expressed a single type of drive or defense. A multitude of case reports show that individuals have used self-destruction for a wide variety of reasons, but by and large our theoretical views do not take this variety into account. My contention is that it may be our attempt to generalize that has been the major factor in our inability to make further progress. If we can classify self-destruction on a different basis, perhaps a more superficial one, we may be able to see further and to improve our therapeutic efforts. For this reason, I suggest the following classification. Each of the classes will be discussed more fully below.

Before proceeding, one assumption should be made explicit. This classification rests on the theoretical basis that human beings have a basic drive to relate to other humans and to get a response from them.[4] Whether we describe this as "libido," "herd instinct" or "gregariousness" does not matter in this context. It is the major orientation of most psychodynamic schools today that psychopathological symptoms result at least in large part from unsatisfactory interpersonal relationships, and are a defense against this lack of satisfaction. We are treating self-destructive behavior as a symptom, and basing our classification upon what the individual is dynamically trying to do, or what is happening to the individual as a result of inadequate relationships.[5]

A Basic Classification of Self-Destructive Behaviors

1) Those who seek death or damage as a way of drawing others into closer psychological contact with them.

2) Those who seek death or damage as a desperate way of changing themselves so that they will be able to relate more closely to others.

3) Those who have eroticized pain so that it is synonymous with emotional contact with others.

4) Those who cannot solve the problem of psychological isolation, and in whom the resultant physiological upset lowers their resistance to physical disease.

5) Those who use drugs or alcohol to bury the pain of isolation or to build a fantasy world in which they are no longer alone.

6) Those who use hostility toward others as a way of reducing their psychological isolation. (When we view this through a longer perspective, with the sure knowledge that hostility

breeds counterhostility ["Those that live by the sword . . ."],
we see the self-destructive quality in this type of behavior.)

It is clear that in a large percentage of self-destructive behavior patterns, the symptom is overdetermined. In any specific case we must expect more than one reason behind the action. This appears to be true of any system of categorizing human motives or behavior.

Those who seek death or damage as a way of drawing others into closer psychological contact with them.

"They will be sorry when I am dead," said Tom Sawyer in a memorable soliloquy. In this category are those who say, "If I cannot have love, I will have pity"—the martyr, the spiteful suicide, many tragedy-prone people. Here are all those who by their actions against themselves aim to mobilize guilt in others, and thereby bind these others more closely to them.

This group may often be seen to make a basic psychodynamic statement: "As a child I was helpless, dependent, and loved. If I can be helpless again, others will love me." In a magical attempt to make others into parental images, they bring about their own dependence and helplessness. In this they are often surprisingly successful. The "tyranny of the weak" can be very strong.

Occasionally, a reaction-formation makes a person in this category feel very strong and powerful rather than weak and helpless, as shown here in a poem by A. E. Housman:

> Good creatures, do you love your lives
> And have you ears for sense?
> Here is a knife like other knives,
> That cost me eighteen pence.
>
> I need but stick it in my heart
> And down will come the sky,
> And earth's foundations will depart
> And all you folk will die.

Those who seek death or damage as a desperate way of changing themselves so that they will be able to relate more closely to others.

Frequently the accident-prone person appears to be reducing his guilt, wiping out the punishment for his hostility by way of an accident. At dynamic levels, his statement seems to be, "If I punish myself for my hostility, I will be cleansed and can live with others." The purpose of this self-destructive behavior is to change something *within* the person. When hostility cannot be controlled or sublimated, the individual feels it may destroy others or his relations with them and he often turns it inward in an intropunitive manner.

The polysurgical addict seems to state dynamically, "There must be some way to remove the still-undiscovered evil that is the source of my isolation." Frequently this behavior is overdetermined. The polysurgical addict finds relationships with doctors, nurses, and sympathetic friends to be the only worthwhile relationships he can establish, since most of his libidinal energies are bound up in his concern about his body.

The attempt to reduce guilt and tension through removing parts of the body is clearly seen in a little-known group who might be called "polydental addicts." Most experienced dentists have seen patients who come in with complaints about a tooth, describing their symptoms quickly and convincingly. At the end of the procedure, the dentist finds, much to his astonishment, that he has drawn out a perfectly sound tooth. Even if this is pointed out, the patient is highly satisfied and departs without any complaints. Some time later, he returns with pain in another healthy tooth.[6]

The "gambler with life" also appears to belong in this general category. These individuals, like the compulsive gambler, make the statement, "If I can get away with this, my fears and guilts are groundless, there is nothing I can be punished for, and I have nothing to fear." Instead of cards or dice, however, they use their environment as an arena. Frequently they do "get away with it"; sometimes they do not.

Speaking generally, this group maintains a fantasy that some "fault" for their isolation lies within themselves and is preventing contact with others. After going through an accident, an operation, or some other self-destructive behavior, they hope to be able to answer their inner accuser with the words used by the Jew of Malta to answer his outer ones: "But that was in another country . . ." (i.e., "Now I am a different person and the accusation is no longer valid."). In the code of chivalry, as in Japanese *bushido*, one can recover one's rightful status and relationships by destroying oneself with a hopeless charge at an overwhelming enemy. This group appears to be engaged in dynamically similar activity.

Those who have eroticized pain so that for them it is synonymous with emotional contact with others.

This group is well known. The psychodynamics of the masochist have been extensively explored, and so widely described that they hardly bear repetition here. For masochists, pain has become symbiotic with love; pain and suffering are not an end in themselves, but a way of reaching sexual release and attaining contact with others. Masochism is a pathological way of loving, of relating to others.

Those who cannot solve the problem of psychological isolation, and in whom the resultant physiological upset lowers their resistance to physical disease.

That psychological tensions can cause disturbances in the body's hormonal and chemical balances has been proven beyond any doubt. Today the diseases we generally call "psychosomatic" also fall into this class. These are not conversion symptoms that symbolically act out unconscious attitudes, but are the resultant physicochemical malfunctions caused by psychological stress.[7]

We frequently consider psychosomatic disease to be a result of self-destructive forces, as if the physical damage were due to an instinctual acting out. It appears that when we do this, we are confusing two separate phenomena with these changes in body chemistry and their resultant physical damage. The first of these phenomena is that the physically damaged person frequently finds that his illness gives him new and effective ways to relate to others; solves some of his interpersonal conflicts; and in general brings him psychological satisfactions as secondary gains. In evaluating the psychosomatically ill patient, we are likely, by a *post hoc, propter hoc* reasoning, to assume that this connection was there *before* the illness, and therefore caused it.

The second of these phenomena is the confusion of the symbolic *meaning* of the illness or symptoms with its *cause*. We analyze the unconscious meaning of the illness or symptom and thereby treat it *as if it were* a conversion symptom. All dramatic aspects of our body or of our behavior take on multiple symbolic meanings, and the physical symptom is no exception. However, when we analyze the meanings and unconscious symbolism of the psychosomatic symptom, we should be clear that we are not going to "cure" that symptom. At best, we may remove some of the psychological pain it causes, or remove a functional overlay that will then permit us to evaluate the results of other treatment methods.[8]

What I am trying to say here is that psychosomatic disease has often been considered an outgrowth of self-destructive drives. However, closer examination demonstrates that this characterization is not quite valid. The disease may also provide a solution to interpersonal conflicts. It almost certainly will take on symbolic meaning for the patient, but it is fundamentally "caused" by his emotional stress and lack of satisfactions, not primarily by his urges to destroy himself.

Those who use drugs or alcohol to bury the pain of isolation or to build a fantasy world in which they are not alone.

> Could man be drunk forever
> With liquor love, or fights,
> Lief should I rouse at morning
> And lief lie down of nights.
>
> But men at whiles are sober
> And think by fits and starts,
> And when they think, they fasten
> Their hands upon their hearts.

A. E. Housman

In Eugene O'Neill's powerful play *The Iceman Cometh*, we see a group of alcoholics who have retreated from their failures into a fantasy world where each reinforces the other's illusions. All the major protagonists were once part of other groups from which they received human contact and affection. For one reason or another, they lost their relationships with these groups and retreated in pain into a lotus land in which they talk of returning to their old status, but would never dream of doing so. Into this stabilized dream world comes Hickey, who manipulates each of them into trying to return to their pre-alcoholic relationships. As Hickey disrupts their dream world, liquor no longer has the power to ease the pain of their loneliness and hurt pride. "Hickey, Hickey, why did you take the kick out of the whiskey?" cries one of them. In the end all their attempts fail, and they turn on Hickey in a fury.

This play presents a clear exposition of one form of self-destructive activity. In the pain of isolation, some individuals retreat from the world completely. They abandon the reality they find so painful and turn to the unreal inner world in which their worth is unquestioned, and in which they are loved and respected. Here they are omnipotent. Tennyson, in his poem "The Lotus Eaters," writes:

> In the hollow Lotus-land, to live and lay
> reclined
> On the hills like Gods together, careless of
> mankind.

However, reality cannot be denied by mortals. In the stronger and stronger denials they must make to maintain their illusions, these individuals must inevitably ignore or negate their other needs. (The physiological effects of alcohol or drugs undoubtedly accelerate their destruction.) Their behavior leads toward damage to wider and wider areas of themselves as consistently as if this growing damage were dynamically determined. As with psychosomatic disease, however, the self-destruction is a by-product of the process rather than a planned end.

Those who use hostility toward others as a way of reducing their psychological isolation.

That human groups are generally more well-knit in the face of an outside threat is well known.[10] We know also that hostility, per se, *is* a relationship, and for many individuals it is far preferable to none. No man is truly alone when he has an enemy.[11]

However, when one looks beyond the immediate conflict it becomes clear that, at least in our modern age, the hostile stance is a suicidal one. And yet it persists in tremendous segments of the world population. We are forced to ask the meaning of this important class of self-destructive behavior.

It would be tempting, indeed, to explain this phenomenon as the result of self-destructive drives. We speak of "the mad rush toward annihilation" of Hitler's Reich, of the world "dashing toward total destruction," and of the obviously suicidal fact that we continue to test and develop more and more thermonuclear weapons.

However, strangely enough, there seems to be no such mass suicidal intent. We cannot find a basic drive toward racial or cultural extinction even in our most pathologically disordered patients.[12] In addition, it would be fair to say that every important human drive and psychodynamic technique ever uncovered in the study of psychology has been foretold in our rich background of myth and literature. Nowhere in this mass of intuitive knowledge do we see evidence of drives toward racial or cultural extinction. Further, when we examine the individual who has been engaged in mass-destruction (i.e., Kelley's or Miale's psychiatric studies of Nazi war criminals), there seems to be clear evidence that their drives were not self-destructive at all. Rather, they were driven by the desires for status, aggrandizement, and all the symbols of membership in groups.

Reluctantly, perhaps, we seem forced to the conclusion that we need no concept of a death instinct to explain this group of "hostility phenomena." Instead, Occam's Razor makes us tentatively accept the simpler hypothesis that these phenomena may be effects of man's confused attempts to be part of a group and to achieve its status symbols and lasting security.

From a somewhat different viewpoint, and with beautiful insight, Edna St. Vincent Millay writes:

> Sweeter was loss than silver coins to spend,
> Sweeter was famine than the belly filled;

Better than blood in the vein was the blood spilled;
Better than corn and healthy flocks to tend
And a tight roof and acres without end
Was the barn burned and the mild creatures killed,
And the back aging fast, and all to build:
For then it was, his neighbor was his friend.
Then for a moment the averted eye
Was turned upon him with benignant beam,
Defiance faltered, and derision slept;
He saw as in a not unhappy dream
The kindly heads against the horrid sky
And scowled, and cleared his throat and spat, and wept.[13]

Conclusion

In discussing these six classes of self-destructive behavior, the purpose of this appendix has been to show something of the variety of motives. To deal with all behavior of this sort as an outgrowth of a death instinct is apparently too general an approach; to deal with each act as individual appears to be too specific.

There should be no assumption that the conclusions reached here present any sort of final answer. I have merely focused on the question, "What is the individual trying to do when he is engaged in self-destructive behavior?" This approach, which answers the question in terms of interpersonal relationships, and the hypotheses presented here, may or may not be valid. The question is the important thing; if we can accept it as a valid and crucial one, we may have faith that science will find answers that will enable us to offer therapeutic intervention. It is my hope such intervention will apply not only to individual psychotherapy, but also to the larger picture.

Appendix Bibliography

1. Alexander, F., "The Need for Punishment and the Death Instinct." *Int. J. PSA*, 10, 1929, 256-269.

2. Alinsky, S., *Reveille for Radicals*, N.Y., Harper, 1942.

3. Durkheim, E., *Suicide, A Study in Sociology*, Glencoe, Ill., Free Press, 1951.

4. Eissler, K. R., *The Psychiatrist and the Dying Patient*, N.Y., International Univ. Press, 1955.

5. Federn, P., "The Reality of the Death Instinct, Especially in Melancholia," *PSA Rev*. 19, 1932, 129-151.

6. Fenechel, O., *The Psychoanalytic Theory of Neuroses*, N.Y., Norton, 1945, 437.

7. Freud, S., *Beyond the Pleasure Principle*, London, Int. PSA Press, 1922.

8. Groddeck, G., *The Book of The It*, N.Y., Nerv. Ment. Dis. Publ. Co., 1928.

9. Jelliffe, Smith Ely, "The Death Instinct in Somatic and Psychopathology." *PSA Rev*. 20, 1933, 121-132.

10. Kubie, Lawrence S., "A Critical Analysis of the Concept of a Repetition Compulsion," *Int. J. PSA*. 20, 1939, 390, 402.

11. LeShan, L., "The Safety Prone, An Approach to the Accident Free Person," *Psychiatry* 4, 1952, 465-469.

12. LeShan, L., "Some Aspects of the Positive Value of Hostility." *Amer. Psychologist* 13, 1958, 118-119.

13. Marbe, K., *Praktische Psychologie der Unfaelle und Betriebschaede*, Berlin, R. Oldenbourg, 1926.

14. Menninger, K., *Man Against Himself*, N.Y., Harcourt, 1938.

15. Millay, Edna St. Vincent, *Collected Sonnets of...*, N.Y., Harper, 1941.

16. Spielrein, S., "Die Destrucktion als Ursache des Werdens," *J. der PSA*. 4, 1912, 89.

17. Stekel, W., "Beitrage zur Traumentung," *J. der PSA*. 1, 1909, 489.

18. Symons, N. J., "Does Masochism Necessarily Imply the Existence of a Death Instinct?" *Intl. J. PSA* 8, 1927, 39-46.

19. Zilboorg, G., "Considerations on Suicide, With Particular Reference to That of the Young," *Amer. J. Orthopsych*. 7, 1937, 115-31.

Appendix Notes

1. Even if a war were fought between two modern countries and atomic weapons were *not* used (a far-fetched idea at best), the presence of so many atomic energy-generating plants all over the modern world would pretty much guarantee the occurrence of a large number of nuclear accidents, most of which would make Chernobyl look like a picnic in the park. There are literally thousands of major atomic energy plants all over the modern world and they will not be spared from bombing or missile attacks. Whether the bombs that fall are "smart" or "dumb," some will hit these extremely vulnerable giants and spill their ten-thousand-year deaths into the air we *must* breathe.

2. Historically, the phalanx was the perfect offensive weapon until the flexibility of the legion proved such a good defense that the phalanx became outmoded. The legion lasted until the development of stir-ruped cavalry. Cavalry, both light and heavy, became the perfect offensive weapon until the development of massed archers behind stake, wagon, or palisade defenses. Massed infantry was replaced by artillery. The trench and machine gun became the perfect defense until the development of armored vehicle tactics. This very brief and extremely superficial overview simply points out that no defense lasts. The tremendous triple walls of Constantinople, widely regarded as impregnable, were quickly breached by new artillery in 1453. The Dutch fort of Eben Emael, which was the finest development in modern fortifications and also believed impregnable to assault, was taken by the new German airborne troops in one day in 1940. Anyone who thinks a workable defense against missile delivery systems of atomic weapons can be built and not be obsolete within a few years at most, simply knows nothing about either history or the present rate of advancement of scientific technology.

3. Since the major work in self-destructive behavior of which I am aware has been done by scholars working from a psychoanalytic orientation, it is from this literature that I have chiefly drawn. The major contributions of statistical sociologists such as Durkheim and Marbe I have briefly referred to where it seemed relevant.

4. This concept has been discussed, particularly from the viewpoint of modern sociologists, earlier in this book. See chapter one. However, it has also been recognized clearly in the psychoanalytic literature. Freud, in his *On Narcissism*, wrote: "In the last analysis we must love in order not to fall ill and must fall ill when, in consequence of frustration, we cannot love." Paul Federn put it even more strongly: "All that is living must be loving so as not to die."

5. The well-known success of Alcoholics Anonymous in treating one form of self-destructive behavior may well be due to the meaningfulness of the relationships that this organization establishes for the alcoholic. In

the experience of the writer, self-destructive behavior ceases when psychotherapy has helped the patient to organize new and successful ways of relating to others.

6. This concept was first described to the writer by Paul Krooks, D.D.S.

7. "Functional changes due to 'toxic' influences, that is, to changes of the chemistry of the unsatisfied and dammed up person, are not necessarily identical with changes caused by an unconscious use of these functions for instinctual purposes." (Fenechel, p. 437)

8. Other aspects of psychotherapy can certainly ease the psychological stresses that lead to physiological malfunctions. When this is done, it often happens that the pathological processes stop and the symptoms disappear. However, it is the general reorientation of the individual and the attainment of satisfactions in interpersonal relationships that do this, not the specific analysis of the symptom.

10. The scapegoat technique is as old as history and offers many possibilities for psychological satisfactions. By projecting our guilts, we can allow ourselves to be closer to others. By displacing our angers, we can permit others to be closer to us. And when we have a common enemy, we can be brothers. War, as well as politics, makes strange bedfellows.

11. This point is presented in more detail in my paper entitled "Some Aspects of the Positive Value of Hostility."

12. Very often the reverse is true. The disordered patient frequently feels that he is a disgrace and a defilement to the human race. It would be startling to find a patient who believed, at deep personality levels, that his species was a disgrace to him.

It may be of interest to note that Eissler, in a wise and perceptive book, *The Psychiatrist and the Dying Patient*, has pointed out that there is no representation of the individual's own death in his unconscious. To go farther, there seems to be no representation of the death of his species either. Even the science fiction writers who have occasionally dealt with this theme have handled it as an accidental (or inevitable) by-product of man's inability to love.

13. Millay, Edna St. Vincent, *Collected Sonnets of...*, Harper, N.Y., 1941.

Notes

INTRODUCTION

4   Richardson, L. F., *The Statistics of Deadly Quarrels*, Boxwood, Pacific Grove, California, 1960.

5   Blainey, G., *The Causes of War*, Free Press, N.Y., 1973.

The people who decried war for twenty years after the last one were correct in all they said. But they uttered their protests (as always) against war—as if war were a person itself or a race of people—against men (e.g. against themselves). . . . They accounted war such an abomination that few so-called decent Americans could look at their advertisements and still pluck up their courage to insist that, for all the peacemakers said against war, its causes are still highly alive—even in their own breasts.

Wylie, P., *Generation of Vipers*, Rinehart and Co., N.Y., 1942, p. 257.

5   International tribunals set up to prevent war have been known all through history. In the nineteenth century they were widely employed. In 1843, a great peace conference was held in London. The leading figures of Europe—Garibaldi, Disraeli, Cobden, Peel, Victor Hugo, Napoleon III—were deeply involved in this effort. A "Peace Bureau" was established and people all over the world gave millions to the cause. The czar of Russia, commander-in-chief of the largest army in the world, summoned a congress in The Hague to set up a world court.

Their ideas and activities came to nothing. The forces inherent in human life that lead to war were far too strong.

Ludwig, E. "War and Peace," in Beard, C. A. (ed.) *Whither Mankind*, Longmans Green, N.Y., 1928, p. 53

6   Angell, N., *The Great Illusion: A Study of the Relation of Military Power in Nations to their Economic and Social Advantage*, G. P. Putnam's Sons, N.Y., 1910.

7   Koestler, A., *Janus*, Random House, N.Y., 1978.

7   Herodotus, *The Histories* (A. de Selincourt, Tr.), Penguin Books, Harmondsworth, Middlesex, England, 1954, p. 13ff.

8   Herodotus, op. cit., p. 212.

8   Thucydides, *The Peloponnesian Wars* (R. Warner, Trans.), Penguin Books, Harmondsworth, Middlesex, England, 1954, p. 210.

8   Freud, S., "Why War?" *Collected Papers*, Vol. 4, The Hogarth Press, London, 1949.

8   It has also been pointed out that it is not necessarily true that the aggressive behavior of nations bears any relation to the aggressive behavior of their citizens. A nation of submissive robots can be led into war more easily than a nation of aggressive individualists. (Niebuhr, R., *The Irony of American History*, Scribners, N.Y., 1952, p. 84ff.)

9   Livy, *The Early History of Rome* (A. de Selincourt, Tr.), Penguin Books, Harmondsworth, Middlesex, England, 1960, p. 81.

9   Thucydides, op. cit., p. 78.

12   The narrowness of different social scientists' viewpoints makes dealing with broader problems such as war far more difficult.

> To the social anthropologist, the individual is lost in structure, emerging, where he must, merely as a social role; to the cultural anthropologist, the individual is baked in a 'cake of custom' . . . following the dictates of established and sacred tradition; to the psychological anthropologist, he or she is stamped in the mold of traditional upbringing.

Goldschmidt, W., "Personal Motivation and Institutional Conflict." In Foster, M. L., and Rubinstein, R. A., *Peace and War: Cross Cultural Perspectives*, Transaction Books, New Brunswick, New Jersey, 1986, p. 3.

12   Before World War I Freud attributed aggression to the frustration of the sexual instincts. After World War I and its disillusioning carnage, Freud attributed it to an "innate, independent, instinctual disposition in mankind." (in Matson, F., *The Idea of Man*, Delacorte, N.Y., 1976, p. 36.)

Freud further wrote in his *An Outline of Psychoanalysis* (W. W. Norton, N.Y., 1949, p. 20), "After long doubts and vacillations we have decided to assume the existence of only two basic instincts, *Eros* and *The Destructive Instinct*."

12   Menninger, K., *Love Against Hate*, Harcourt Brace and Co., N.Y., 1942, p. 4.

14   Ardrey, R., *The Hunting Hypothesis*, Atheneum, N.Y., 1976.

14   Voltaire gave one aspect of these "human nature" theories in *Candide*:

CANDIDE: Do you think that men have always massacred one another as they do today?. . .

MARTIN: Do you think that hawks have always eaten pigeons when they could find them?

CANDIDE: Of course I do.

MARTIN: Well, if hawks have always had the same character why should you suppose that men have changed theirs?

14 Lorenz, K., *On Aggression*, Bantam, N.Y., 1966, p. 234ff.

15 In General S. L. A. Marshall's study of the American infantryman in World War II, he found that the major force driving the actual fighting was not destruction of the enemy or anger or hatred, but the desire not to let down the other members of the squad. (Turner, P. R., Pitt, D., et al. *The Anthropology of War and Peace*, Begin and Gateway Publications, Amherst, Mass., 1989, p. xiff.) Other studies confirm this. For example, the definitive study in this area (Merton, R. K., and Lazarfeld, P., *The American Soldier*, Free Press, Glencoe, Ill., Vol. 2, 1950) reports that hatred of the enemy decreased with more combat experience. It was primarily in-group loyalty that kept the fighting going.

15 Koestler, op. cit., p. 60.

15 Montagu, A., *Man Observed*, G. P. Putnam & Sons, N.Y., 1968, p. 190.

15 Montagu, op. cit., p. 192.

15 Fried, M., Harris, M., and Murphy, R., *War: The Anthropology of Armed Conflict and Aggression*, Natural History Press, Garden City, N.Y., 1968.

15 Benedict, R., *Patterns of Culture*, Houghton Mifflin, Boston, 1959 (originally published 1934), p. 12ff.

16 Juvenal, *Sixth Satire*, lines 95-96 (R. Humphries, Tr.), *The Satires of Juvenal*, Indiana University Press, Bloomington, Indiana, 1958.

16 Quoted in Toynbee, A. J., *War and Civilization*, Oxford University Press, Oxford, 1950, p. 26

Toynbee, op. cit., p. 25.

Toynbee, op. cit., p. 25.

Toynbee, op. cit., p. 16.

17 Aron, R., *The Century of Total War*, Beacon Press, Boston, 1955, p. 55ff.

18 Lenin, V. I., *Socialism and War*, 2nd ed., Foreign Language Publishing House, Moscow, 1936 (originally published 1915), p. 10. Quoted in Alcock, N. Z., *The War Disease*, CPRI Press, Oakville, Ontario, 1972, p. 8ff.

18 Luxemburg, R., quoted in Aron, op. cit., p. 57.

18 Otterbain, K. F., *The Evolution of War*, HRAF Press, N.Y., 1970.

19 James, W., *The Pluralistic Universe*, Longmans Green, N.Y., 1909.

19 For example: *The Philosophy of Symbolic Forms* (2 vols.), Yale University Press, New Haven, 1955 (originally published 1921).

19 A far more detailed and comprehensive review of this topic can be found in the works referred to above by Blainey and Aron, as well as in the *Encyclopedia Britannica*. Because these reviews (and others) are so well done, a more in-depth review is not presented here.

CHAPTER ONE

21   Sarton, M., *At Seventy*, Norton, N.Y., 1984, p. 174.

21   "When arms have been taken up, there is no respect for law, human or divine," wrote Hugo Grotius in 1625. Earlier Shakespeare had written:

> The gates of mercy shall be all shut up,
> And the flesh'd soldier, rough and hard of heart,
> In liberty of bloody hand shall range
> With conscience wide as hell . . .
> *(Henry V)*

22   Barnet, R., *The Roots of War*, Penguin, N.Y., 1973, p. 16.

22   Sorokin, P., quoted in Blainey, G., op. cit.

22   Encyclopedia Britannica, 15th ed., Vol. 19, p. 16.

22   The statement that "war is natural" has no meaning, and any comment on it must be mainly speculation as to what those who make it imagine they mean when they repeat the words. Natural to whom, when and under what conditions? "Let dogs delight to bark and bite, it is their nature to." Is it the nature, too, of men of science?

Pollard, A. P., "The War of Nature and a Peace of Mind." *Vincula*, University of London Student's Journal, 14 December 1925, p. 60. Quoted in Montagu, op. cit., p. 276.

23   We have known since Roman times that humanity is the only species that has invented war (*vide* Pliny the Elder). Da Vinci defined man as the only animal that persecutes members of its own species. Montagu, op. cit., pp. 284 and 290.

From *psychological* studies of animals, we have learned only that animals (or computers) can tell us nothing about the psychology of human beings. For a fuller discussion of this, see LeShan, L., *The Dilemma of Psychology*, N.Y., Dutton, 1990.

25   Arendt, H., *The Human Condition*, University of Chicago Press, Chicago, 1958, p. 22.

25   Scott, "The Lay of the Last Minstrel," canto six, in Felleman, H. (ed.), *Best Loved Poems of the American People*, Doubleday, N.Y., 1936, p. 423.

25   Remen, N., from lecture at Symington Cancer Conference, San Francisco, 1991.

26   Only through a meaningful development of his individual childhood with one of the major trends of history can an individual find his ego identity.

The conscious feeling of having a personal identity is based on two simultaneous observations; the immediate perception of one's self-sameness and identity in time: and the simultaneous perception of the fact that others recognize one's sameness and continuity.

Roazen, P., *Erik H. Erikson*, Free Press, N.Y., 1970, pp. 33, 43.

The sociologist George Herbert Mead also wrote of this "double self" in clear, strong terms. Typical of his statements are the following:

The self has reality only as other selves have reality.

The child fashions his own self on the model of other selves. This is not an attitude of imitation, but the self that appears in consciousness must function in conjunction with other selves.

The self, however,is a social individual. It arises out of social conduct.

Miller, D. L. (ed.), *The Individual and The Social Self: The Unpublished Works of G. H. Mead*, University of Chicago Press, Chicago, 1982, pp. 54, 55, 102.

Or, as a widely used textbook in sociology puts it:

A fundamental assumption of sociology is that the self is a product of interaction with others and that it can never develop in a social vacuum. . . . The absence of interaction with others, or even a minimal amount of interaction produces only a shell of a human being.

Alleym, C., *Sociology*, Prentice-Hall, Englewood Cliffs, N.J., 1972, p. 88.

As early as 1912, the sociologist Charles Cooley described the self as a "looking glass self." That suicide rates vary inversely with the degree of integration in a society has been well known since the work of Emile Durkheim in the early 1900s. The tighter the group someone belongs to, the more that person tends to be self-protective and self-preservative.

26   Koestler, op. cit., p. 57ff.

28   Tolstoy, L., *War and Peace* (C. Garnett, Tr.), Modern Library Editions, N.Y., 1979, p. 221.

28   In the face of danger, the autonomic nervous system is called into play and the subsequent outpouring of adrenaline and other endocrine substances sharpens the mind, quickens the pulse, stimulates the imagination and heightens the senses.... Danger can be a transcendent experience providing one finally escapes from it, and in play, one always expects to win.

Clark, M. M., "The Cultural Patterning of Risk Taking Behavior," in: Foster and Rubinstein, op. cit., p. 84.

28   Manchester, W., *Goodbye Darkness: A Memoir of the War*, Little Brown, Boston, 1983, p. 123.

28   Remarque, E. M., *All Quiet on the Western Front* (A. W. Where, Tr.), Little Brown, Boston, 1957, p. 53.

29   Remarque, op. cit., p. 94.

29   Coudert, J., *Advice From a Failure*, Stein and Day, N.Y., 1965, p. 57.

30   In 1915, a convoy of six shiploads of rubber, desperately needed by Germany's war machine, was sent from Southeast Asia to Holland. The French navy intercepted the six freighters and brought them into a French port. Pressure from above resulted in the ships' release, and they proceeded to Holland. The official word was that France accepted the statements on the manifests of the ships that their cargo was destined for the manufacture of contraceptives.

Van Passen, P., *Days of Our Years*, Hillmann-Curl, Inc., N.Y., 1939. See also Upton Sinclair's reports on this kind of activity, particularly in the "Lanny Budd" series.

CHAPTER TWO

33   Becker, E., *Escape From Evil.* Quoted in Keen, S. and Valley-Fox, A., *Your Mythic Journey*, Jeremy Tarcher, Los Angeles, 1989, p. 123.

33   Russell, B., quoted in Abrams, I. (ed.), *The Words of Peace*, Newmarket, N.Y., 1980, p. 11.

33   The widely held view that wars arise out of certain sets of circumstances—arms races, economic conditions, crises, and so forth-resembles more the medieval view that maggots originate from filth than it does truth.

Seabury, P., and Codevilla, A., *War: Ends and Means*, Basic Books, N.Y., 1989, p. 9.

34   Getting into war is not like catching a cold. It is more like catching AIDS. It is not easy.

Seabury and Codevilla, op. cit., p. 45.

35   For a fuller discussion of the differences between various widely used ways of perceiving and experiencing reality, see LeShan, L., *Alternate Realities*, Evans Publishing Co., N.Y., 1976, and LeShan, L., and Margenau, H., *Einstein's Space and Van Gogh's Sky*, MacMillan, N.Y., 1982.

37   The enemy is, needless to say, cruel and hardly human; there is no use in treating him as if he were human.

Perls, F., Hefferline, R. E., and Goodman, P., *Gestalt Therapy*, Bantam, N.Y., 1957, p. 406.

37   May, R., *Power and Innocence*, Delta, N.Y., 1972, p. 166.

38   The figures in fairy tales are not ambivalent—not good and bad at the same time as we all are in reality.

Bettelheim, B., *The Uses of Enchantment*, Random House, N.Y., 1977, p. 9.

38   Quoted in Keen and Valley-Fox, op. cit.

38   Myerson, A., *Speaking of Man*, Knopf, N.Y., 1950, p. 101.

39   Fahey, J., and Armstrong, R., *A Peace Reader*, Paulist Press, N.Y., 1987. An article by J. Garvey ("Murderous Evil: Does Non-Violence Offer a Solution") points out that assertions like "Wars never solve anything" or "All wars are fought to benefit the military-industrial complex" are based on simple misunderstanding and avoid the question of a Hitler or a Dachau.

39   Lorenz, K., op. cit., p. 234.

41   Erikson, E., "Wholeness and Totality," in Bramson, L., and Goethals, G. W. (eds.), *War*, Basic Books, N.Y., 1964, p. 122.

41   Erikson describes everyday sensory reality as "wholeness" and mythic reality as "totality." "Wholeness," he says, is made up of "an assembly of parts, even quite different parts that enter into a fruitful association and organization." Since this assembly has fluid and open boundaries, new ideas and facts may enter in and change the total picture or parts of it.

Totality, as an orientation towards reality, includes an absolute boundary of perception and concepts. Nothing inside must be left outside, nothing that must be outside can be tolerated inside. Totality cannot be changed by new ideas coming from outside or by the development of inner concepts through interaction . . .

Erikson, op. cit., p. 122.

While such realignments may seem to appear suddenly, they develop slowly. Only uncommonly brave and aware people know . . . how strong and systematic are men's *proclivities and potentialities for such realignments*. (Erikson's italics)

Erikson, op. cit., p. 124.

41   Once a hostile image of a total group is formed, all members become identical. We are not in a mythic organization of reality and the image is peculiarly resistant to the onset of contrary evidence. An Oxford student once remarked: "I despise all Americans, but I never met one I didn't like." (Gordon Allport in Cantril, H., *Tensions That Cause Wars*, University of Illinois Press, Urbana, Illinois, 1950, p. 62.)

42   U.S. peace activists during the Vietnam War and, to a lesser degree, the Persian Gulf War found that they could obtain all the psychological benefits of war while protesting against it. They could protect their inner tensions and displace angry feelings against others, with the gov-

ernment being the distant enemy. They could attain intensity and meaning in their lives through their great cause, and the danger presented by the police. They could be part of a band of comrades and attain solid group membership. In short, they could live in a mythic organization of reality, organized around the concept that we shall overcome and live in peace and harmony forever. There is no imputation of their sincerity nor of the fact that—at least in the Vietnam War—their cause was far superior to that of the government in terms of morality and practicality.

42   Mircea Eliade, in *Myth and Reality*, Dover, N.Y., 1963, has pointed out that mythic thought gives us models of how we *ought* to behave. It gives us ideal examples. We feel good when we shift into the mythic mode and identify ourselves with the heroic. We are always the good ones, and the forces of nature—God or whatever—are always on our side. We expect to win, despite the inevitable hardships we experience.

42   Whitehead, A. N., quoted in Price, L., (ed.), *Dialogues With Alfred North Whitehead*, Little, Brown, Boston, 1954, p. 296.

CHAPTER THREE

45   The previous pages of this chapter are a paraphrase of material from LeShan, L., *Alternate Realities. op. cit.*

45   Until the work of Cassirer, mythic thought was considered "explained" if its origin in various human needs was made plausible. Now we see that this sort of explanation is not adequate. Mythic thought is now seen as one way human beings organize reality. It is not, as was previously believed, a *distortion* of reality, but rather another widely used means of constructing reality, useful for some purposes, not useful for others. In the studies of both thought and language, scientific (sensory reality) thought was generally seen as the "correct" way and mythic thought was an error and mistake, ". . . a product of ignorance. But the whole realm of mythical concepts is too great a phenomena to be counted as a 'mistake' due to the absence of logically recorded facts. Mere ignorance should be agnostic—empty or negative—not exciting and irrepressible. . . . Language, the symbolization of thought, exhibits two entirely different modes of thought. Yet in both modes the mind is powerful and creative."

Langer, S., Introduction to Cassirer, E., *Language and Myth* (S. Langer, Tr.), Dover, N.Y., 1953, p. viii.

It must be remembered that there is no sharp dividing line between the mythic and the scientific methods of organizing reality. They shade into each other.

47   The Russian noblemen of the early 1800s called Napoleon "The Antichrist."

47   Bramson and Goethals, op. cit. p. 264.

48   Seabury and Codevilla, op. cit., p. 52.

Since we are in a situation of absolute good opposing absolute evil, we agree with General Ludendorff of the German army in World War I when he wrote:

> All the means to weaken an enemy nation become legitimate. By killing women and children, for example, one destroys the future mothers and eventual defenders of the country.

Quoted in Young, R., *Wars Must Cease*, Macmillan, N.Y., 1935, p. 17.

48   Seabury and Codevilla, op. cit., p. 230.

49   It was the psychoanalyst Karen Horney who pointed out that when we are unreasonably angry at someone, we should ask ourselves whether we believe we had some sort of contract with them that they violated.

49   Even in peacetime, questioning the accepted mythology usually gets a strong response. Anna, the daughter of the philosopher Ernst Cassirer, was at school in Berlin when she was 13. Assigned an essay on the Nibelungenlied (one of the great German myths), she took an original approach. She wrote that the person usually considered the hero, Siegfried, did not seem very brave to her as he was protected by magical powers and thus invulnerable. She said that to her the real hero was Hagen, who is usually considered the villain. The teachers were outraged and insisted her father come to the school. He did and they showed him the essay. His response, that he did not particularly agree or disagree but felt very glad that his daughter had a mind of her own, further outraged them. They expelled his daughter at the first opportunity.

(Before the expulsion, however, another essay was assigned. Cassirer himself wrote this and his daughter brought it in as her own. They gave her a failing mark. Cassirer then wrote them a note thanking them for a new experience. He wrote that he had never in his life flunked an essay until after he became a full professor at the University of Berlin!)

49   Silone, I., quoted in Crossman, R. (ed.), *The God that Failed*, Gateway, N.Y., 1987 (originally published 1949).

50   Mead, M., *And Keep Your Powder Dry*, William Morrow, N.Y., 1942, p. 156.

50   Falwell, J., quoted in Deikman, *The Wrong Way Home*, Beacon, Boston, 1990, p. 105.

51   Benedict, R., op. cit., p. 8.

51   The Crusades were probably the best examples of a mythic war.

> The Crusaders set out under this or that baron, but their actual leader was God himself and the barons were His temporal lieutenants. . . . The army was led by Jesus Christ himself.

Oldenbourg, Z., *The Crusades*, Random House, N.Y., 1966, p. 45.

Half a century ago scientists used to evaluate their theories and theoretical concepts by asking the question: Is the theory or theoretical concept, true or false? Since the days of Henri Poincaré the notion has gradually gained ascendancy that the aforementioned criteria is not the proper one. Nowadays we do not ask whether a given concept is true or false. We ask: Is it convenient or inconvenient, is it useful or not.

Rashevsky, N., in Frank, P. G., *The Validation of Scientific Theories*, Beacon, Boston, 1954.

The fact that we can never know what reality is, is clarified by the following. A guess is made as to how things are or work. We wish to compare it to the 'truth.' What does this mean? We cannot even guess. What a comparison would mean is completely unclear.

Einstein, A., and Infeld, L., *The Evolution of Physics*, Simon and Schuster, N.Y., 1938, p. 35.

Since the work of Max Planck on quantum mechanics early in this century, physics has changed its orientation from a search for the truth of "how things are" to a search for the most useful ways to construe and define reality. The search for absolute reality has been abandoned and replaced by a quest for new and more useful ways to describe our observations. The physicist-philosopher Henry Margenau put it:

. . . absolute reality is ultra-perceptory and hence is of no interest in science. For no amount of observation could ever verify absoluteness. The view here taken might be described as affirming *dynamic* or *constructive* reality, and I fail to see that it is even aesthetically less satisfying than the postulate of an absolute, static reality. The physicist does not discover, he creates his universe.

Margenau, H., "Metaphysical Elements in Physics," *Review of Modern Physics*, Vol. 13, No. 3, July 1941, pp. 176-189.

Margenau's last sentence sums up the modern viewpoint in science. We organize the world into different realities and the test is of usefulness and fruitfulness rather than absolute truth. The physicist Arthur Eddington tried to make this clear with an example:

In my observatory there is a telescope which condenses the light of a star on a film of sodium in a photo-electric cell. I rely on the classical theory to conduct the light through the lenses and focus it on the cell: then I switch to the quantum theory to make the light fetch out electrons from the sodium film to be collected in an electrometer. If I happen to transpose the two theories, the quantum theory convinces me that the light will never get concentrated in the cell, and the classical theory shows that it is powerless to extract the electron if it does get in. I have no logical reason for not using the theories this way round, only experience teaches me that I must not. Sir William Bragg was right when he said that we use the Classical Theory on Mondays, Wednesdays and Fridays, and the Quantum Theories on Tuesdays, Thursdays and Saturdays.

Quoted in Tyrrell, G. N. M., *Grades of Significance*, Rider and Co., London, 1930, p. 56.

56   Harris, L., quoted in Deikman, op. cit., p. 88.

57   Orwell, G., *Homage to Catalonia*, quoted in Dyson, F., *Weapons and Hope*, Harper and Row, N.Y., 1984, p. 129.

57   Koestler, A., quoted in Crossman, op. cit., p. 23.

57   Seabury and Codevilla, op. cit., p. 52.

58   Woodward, C. V., and Muhlenfeld, E. (eds.), *The Private Mary Chesnut: The Unpublished Civil War Diaries*, Oxford University Press, Oxford, 1984. Her poem may have been overdramatic and bad poetry besides. However, Rupert Brooke, who often wrote far better poetry, expressed much the same thing—at least as high and mythic a sentiment—from the viewpoint of 1914 as she had from the viewpoint of 1861:

> Now God, be thanked who has matched us with His hour
> And caught our youth and wakened us from sleeping;
> With hand made sure, clear eye, and sharpened power,
> To turn, as swimmers into cleanness leaping,
> Glad from a world grown old and cold and weary,
> Leave the sick hearts that honor could not move,
> And half-men with their dirty songs and dreary,
> And all the little emptiness of love!

To quote Paul Fussell,

> That way of looking at a war would almost persuade the giver of thanks to celebrate the Central Powers for violating Belgian neutrality, thus providing the means by which God might work his redemptive operations.

Fussell, P., *Wartime*, Oxford University Press, Oxford, 1989, p. 130.

58   de la Mare, W., "How Sleep the Brave." In Clarke, H. C., *A Treasury of War Poetry,*, Houghton-Mifflin, N.Y., 1917, p. 227.

CHAPTER FOUR

59   A widely seen United States poster in 1917 said "Hell is too good for the Hun."

59   Who will win if the commander of one army is God and the commander of the other army is Satan?

      Saddam Hussein in first month of Persian Gulf War.

59   Exploration in this field also demands courage. We must take chances, not always be moderate, and avoid overconcern with fairness. In Elinor Wylie's words:

> The worst and best are both inclined
> to snap like vixens at the truth:
> But, O, beware the middle mind that
> purrs and never shows a tooth.

60   Royle, T., *War Report*, Mainstream Publications, Worcester, England, 1987, p. 24.

61   Tuchman, B. *The March of Folly*, Knopf, N.Y. 1984.

62   No TV program or newspaper reported, to my knowledge, that during and for at least several months after the Persian Gulf War, Saudi Arabia refused to let any U.S. senators enter the country if their passports showed that they had visited Israel.

64   We have not even to risk the adventure alone; for the heroes of all time have gone before us; the labyrinth is thoroughly known; we have only to follow the thread of the hero-path.

Campbell, J., *The Hero with a Thousand Faces* (rev. ed.), Princeton University Press, Princeton, N.J., 1990

The following anecdote was told to me by Ethical Culture Society leader Algernon Black: A child listened to a story told by the religious leader John Lovejoy Elliot. After it was over the child asked, "Is that story true?" "No," replied Elliot, "but it is truer than true." The child was satisfied.

Children know that while fairy stories are unreal they are not untrue. And we know that too. In World War I, it would not have mattered if someone could have proved to the American public that the Germans did not carry babies spitted on their bayonets as they marched to battle and did not habitually rape Belgian nuns. Having shifted to a mythical organization of reality, we *knew* the Germans were evil, and if these tales were not true, then worse was and we simply did not yet know the details.

65   Sometimes the person directing a war will attempt a sub-classification of enemies into the "temporarily on a wrong track" and the "hopelessly evil." Thus, in the first attempt at arms control (1134 A.D.), the crossbow was prohibited for use against Christians since it was inhumane, but allowed against Muslims. This prohibition failed as the distinction could only work when the leader had complete control over his troops and their fighting; at this time, the pope did not.

CHAPTER FIVE

71   Wylie, P., *Opus 21*, Pocket Books, N.Y., 1958, p. 55.

71   Wilson, S., *Ice Brothers*, Avon, N.Y., 1979, p. I.

The psychiatrist Karl Menninger wrote in 1938 of the attitude toward the obviously coming war that he observed in Europe: "The spectacle of almost joyous preparation for mass suicide as is now in progress. . . ."

Menninger, K. A., *Man Against Himself*, Harcourt Brace and Co., N.Y., 1938, p. 46.

72   Cordier, A. W. and Foote, W. (eds.), *The Quest for Peace*, Columbia University Press, N.Y., 1965, p. 59.

72   *Encyclopedia Britannica*, 15th ed., vol. 19, pp. 543-44.

72   Sorokin, op. cit., p. 3.

74   Coles, R., "The Need for Scapegoats Causes War," in Bender, D. L., and Leone, B. (eds.), *War and Human Nature*, Greenhaven Press, St. Paul, Minn., 1983, p. 60.

74   Paradoxically people may go to war because they are starved for love, for "belonging" . . .

Angyal, A., *Foundations for a Science of Personality*, Viking, N.Y., 1941, p. 212.

Hatred is the most accessible of all unifying agents. We do not look for allies when we love, but we always look for allies when we hate.
           Eric Hoffer

Quoted in Setter, I., *Man: The Reluctant Brother*, Fieldstone Press, N.Y., 1967, p. 121.

. . . one sees in times of catastrophe, war, earthquakes, floods, shipwrecks, etc. . . . there is sympathy, compassion, a sort of love between men who hated each other the day before.

Simenon, G., *When I Was Old*, Harcourt Brace Jovanovich, N.Y., 1971, p. 68.

74   Alinsky, S., *Reveille for Radicals*, Harper & Co., N.Y., 1942.

75   January 14, 1991, "Nightline," ABC.

75   Dyson, op. cit., p. 18.

76   Seabury and Codevilla, op cit., p. 186.

76   Menninger, op cit. p. 4.

76   Case reported to me by the psychotherapist Ann Cassirer Applebaum, 1989.

77   Coles, R., op. cit.

77 Stevenson, R., in Dyson, op. cit., p. 157.

77 . . . many among the most civilized peoples of the modern world have greeted the onset of war with cries of joy. . . . Many [social scientists] have asked whether there are real satisfactions in war both ancient and modern, which might offer a clue as to why so many peoples have embraced the military experience because it represents life's potentialities raised to the highest power. To ask such questions, however, is to fly in the face of conventional opinion. Today it is not considered polite or reasonable to admit a taste for war . . .

Bramson and Goethals, op. cit., p. 6.

77 James, W., "The Moral Equivalent of War." Reprinted in Bramson and Goethals, op cit., p. 27.

77 Catton, B., *Reflections on the Civil War*, Berkley Books, N.Y., 1982, p. xv.

78 I recall a series of books widely read in America, *The Boy Allies*, about a group of brave, dedicated young soldiers who seemed to have won every battle of World War I, as well as movies such as *Wings* or the many starring John Wayne, Clark Gable, and others. Soldiers were depicted as knights in a great cause, much like the Round Table of King Arthur.

78 My first unforgettable exposure to war was Erich Maria Remarque's *All Quiet on the Western Front*. The author dedicated the book to the memory of a generation "that had been destroyed by war even though it may have escaped its guns." Yet many old people to whom I spoke about the war remembered its outbreak as a time of glory and rejoicing.

Stoesinger, J. G., *Why Nations Go to War*, St. Martin's Press, N.Y., 1974, p. 11.

78 Gray, J. G., *The Warriors*, Harper and Row, N.Y., 1967, p. 44. Gray also writes:

For some of them [combat veterans] the war years were what Dixon Wecter has called "the one great lyric passage in their lives." (p. 28)

Anyone who has lived through an air raid of any magnitude at all knew a quality of excitement scarcely experienced before or since. Fear may have been the dominant feature of such excitement, rarely was it the only ingredient. . . . There is often a surge of vitality and a glimpse of potentialities of what we really are or have been or might become. (p. 14)

79 A southern businessman talking about the drug epidemic:

I always thought that if this civilization ended it would be with the mushroom-shaped cloud, but I never thought we would smoke it or inject it.

November 5, 1989, "Sunday Morning," CBS.

E. M. Forster wrote of the V1 and V2 rockets: "I think they are going to be important psychologically. They bitch the romance of the air—war's last beauty parlor." Quoted in Fussell, op. cit., p. 132.

79   Freud, S., *Civilization and its Discontents*, (first published 1929), in Freud, S., *Civilization, War and Death*, (J. Rickman, Tr.), Hogarth Press, London, 1939.

80   Arthur Koestler reports on the great similarity of the "inner certitude" of the Communist party member "and the closed universe" of the drug addict. Both, he says, live in similar mythic constructions of reality.

Crossman, R., op. cit., p. 53.

80   We are going to have upheavals of violence for as long as experiences of significance are denied people.

May, op. cit., p. 178.

80   Sartre, J. P., *The Age of Reason* (E. Sutton, Tr.), Knopf, N.Y., 1960 (originally published 1945), p. 244.

81   Dobyns, S., *Toting It Up*, quoted in *The New York Times Book Review*, December 12, 1990, p. 8.

81   Stendhal, *The Charterhouse of Parma*, Zodiac Press, 1980, p. 3.

81   Sartre, J. P., *The Reprieve*, Knopf, N.Y., 1966 (originally published 1947), p. 78.

81   One source [of the allure of war] is the attraction of the extreme situation—that is, the risking of all in battle.

May, op. cit., p. 175.

82   Clark, M. M., "The Cultural Patterning of Risk Taking Behavior," in Foster and Rubinstein, op. cit., p. 83.

82   CNN, July 19, 1992.

82   *Time*, August 6, 1990.

82   Before the Persian Gulf War, there were always widespread reports on TV of crimes, fires, and injustice. During the brief war, these disappeared to the degree that anyone watching TV would get the impression the United States was an Eden. After the war, these reports immediately reappeared on TV news programs.

83   Caputo, P., *A Rumor of War*, Ballantine, N.Y.,1977, p. 6.

83   We are thus driven to the unfashionable conclusion that the trouble with our species is not an excess of *aggression*, but an excessive capacity for fanatical *devotion*. Even a cursory glance at history should convince one that individual crimes committed for selfish motives play a quite insignificant part in the human tragedy, compared to the numbers massacred in unselfish loyalty to one's tribe,

nation, dynasty, church, or political ideology, *ad majoram gloria dei*. The emphasis is on unselfish. . . . Homicide for unselfish reasons, at the risk of one's own life, is the dominant phenomenon in history.

Koestler, op. cit., p. 14.

84   Gray, op. cit., p. 124.

84   Brookhouser, F. (ed.), *This Was Your War*, Doubleday, N.Y., 1980, p. 53.

85   Caputo, op. cit., p. xvi.

85   Caputo, op. cit., p. 10.

85   "60 Minutes," September 7, 1991, CBS.

85   Merton and Lazarfeld, op. cit., p. 33ff.

85   . . . loyalty to the group is the essence of fighting morale. The commander who can preserve it and strengthen it knows that all other psychological or physical factors are little in comparison.

Gray, op. cit., p. 40.

85   If one man gets a letter from home, the whole company reads it. What belongs to me belongs to the entire outfit.

Merton and Lazarfeld, op. cit., p. 99.

86   Symons, J., "Notes from Another Country," from Sinclair, H. (ed.), *The War Decade: An Anthology of the 1940s*, Hamish Hamilton, Publisher, London, 1989, p. 76.

86   (January 1941)
Citizens have been asked and have shown a willingness to form communal fire-fighting squads, which are to take turns patrolling the streets, armed with the keys of absent neighbors so that fires in empty houses can be quickly reached and controlled. For the reserved and suspicious British, this represents a step forward, not only in civic discipline but also in the un-English mateyness which is one of the few pleasant things to come out of the war so far.

Editors, *The New Yorker* magazine, *The New Yorker Book of War Pieces*, Bloomsbury Publishing, London, 1947.

87   See for example LeShan, L., "Loss of Cathexes as a Common Psychodynamic Characteristic of Cancer Patients," *Psychological Reports*, Vol. 2, 1956, pp. 183-193.

88   Freud, S., from *Civilization, War and Death*, p. 2.

88   Deikman, op. cit., p. 6.

89   Quoted in Gramling, O., *Free Men Are Fighting*, Farrar and Rinehart, N.Y., 1942, p. 165.

89   Farwell, B., *Mr. Kipling's Army*, W. W. Norton, N.Y., 1982, p. 93.

89   It is one of the commonplaces of popular sociological observation

that the military peoples, castes, and class are more apt to win more admiration from us than their neighbors who earn their living by occupations which do not extend to the risking of one's own life in the attempt to take someone else's.

Toynbee, op. cit., p. 12.

90 William James wrote in "The Moral Equivalent of War" that we must find a way to bring these "military virtues" into civilian life if we are ever to be able to prevent war.

90 Fussell, op. cit.

91 Mead, op. cit., p. 140.

91 Gray, op. cit., p. 135.

97 Catton, op. cit., p. 61ff.

97 Manchester, op. cit., p. 391.

97 Farwell, op. cit., 1983.

97 . . . war indicates a throwback . . . on the part of people who can no longer stand the exacting strain of life in groups, with all the necessities for compromise, give-and-take, live-and-let-live, understanding and sympathy that such life demands, and with all the complexities of adjustment involved . . . the ability of war to commend the loyalty and interests of the entire underlying population rests partly upon its peculiar psychological reactions: it provides an outlet and an emotional release. . . . For war is the supreme drama of a completely mechanized society; and it has an element of advantage that puts it high above all the other preparatory forms of mass-sport in which the attitudes of war are mimicked: war is real . . . and it may bring it [reality] to the remotest spectators as well as to the gladiators in the center . . .

Mumford, L., *Technics and Civilization*, Harcourt, Brace and World, Inc., N.Y., 1934, p. 308ff.

CHAPTER SIX

99 Bender and Leone, op. cit., p. 13.

100 Woodham-Smith, C., *The Reason Why*, Times, Inc., N.Y., 1962, p. 144.

100 Tuchman, op. cit.

101 Tuchman, op. cit., p. 234, 273.

101 Arnold Toynbee discusses in detail the slowness of change in military organizations in his *War and Civilization*, op. cit.

102 Thucydides, op. cit., p. 55.

102   Thucydides, op. cit., p. 15.

102   Livy, op. cit., p. 81.

102   Herodotus, op. cit., p. 18.

102   The act of raising and paying armies may well be the most typical act that any regime performs.

        Seabury and Codevilla, op. cit., p. 270.

103   *Encyclopedia Britannica*, 15th ed., vol. 14, pp. 723-726.

104   Pearson, L., quoted in Abrams, I. op. cit., p. 121.

104   Adams, H., *The Education of Henry Adams*, Houghton-Mifflin Co., Boston, 1971 (originally published 1918), p. 98.

CHAPTER SEVEN

107   Holmes, O. W., quoted in Murphy, G., *Human Potentialities*, Basic Books, N.Y., 1958, p. vi.

107   Once more I beg you all to tear away the veil of sentimental mysticism through which you have looked at war and try to see it as it really is. The words which you have associated with it for so many years: "victory," "defeat," "indemnities," "non-combatants"; these words have now lost their meaning; just as the word "war" has lost its meaning. It is no longer war. It is as far removed from the Napoleonic Wars as they were from a boxing match. This new thing which you are asked to renounce is a degradation which would soil the beasts, a lunacy which would shame the madhouse. In renouncing it, you will be renouncing nothing which History has accepted or Poetry idealized, nothing in which your countries have found profit or your countrymen glory.

        A. A. Milne, quoted in Young, op. cit., p. 37.

107   To repeat the earlier conclusions of this book—the promise of war offers a clean conscience, full membership in a group, meaningfulness to one's actions and intensity in one's life, and a chance to change to an easier, less stressful, more magical way of organizing reality. Where else can you get all that at once?

108   Romain Rolland's fictional character Clerambault was extremely antimilitarist. Clerambault was reading a mobilization poster in 1914 and feeling very much against the war. Then a military band went by and he noticed to his astonishment and dismay that he had fallen in step with the music and was marching behind the band.

108   "War is unknown to some of the most primitive men—the Great Basin Shoshone Indians, for example, who are about as close to a biological 'state of nature' as one can find."

Barnet, R. J., *Roots of War*, Penguin, N.Y., 1973, p. 5.

109   Seabury and Codevilla, op. cit., p. 5.

109   Blainey, op. cit., p. 25.

109   After World War I, Winston Churchill wrote: "Torture and cannibalism were the only two expedients that the civilized, scientific, Christian states had been able to deny themselves; and these were of doubtful utility."

Young, op. cit., p. 16.

110   It was the philosopher Friedrich Schelling who first recognized mythic methods as "an essential modality of human thought."

Cassirer, E., *The Philosophy of Symbolic Forms* (R. Mannheim, Tr.), Yale University Press, New Haven, 1953 (originally published 1925), p. 4.

111   "I don't think for a second that defeating him [Saddam Hussein] will mean the advent of a new world order. But I am convinced that failing to beat him will make the present world order far more perilous."

Caputo, P., "War Torn," *New York Times Magazine*, February 24, 1991, p. 36.

112   That Europe was not to be a Mohammedan culture was decided by the battle of Tours and later also by further military conflict at the siege of Vienna. The battle of Marathon decided the direction of European culture at least to the present time. Other examples abound.

113   Then it's Tommy this, an' Tommy that, an' "Tommy, 'ows yer soul?"
But it's "Thin red line of 'eroes" when the drums begin to roll
—The drums begin to roll, my boys, the drums begin to roll,
O it's "Thin red line of 'eroes" when the drums begin to roll.

For it's Tommy this, an' Tommy that, and "Chuck him out, the brute!"
But it's "Saviour of 'is country" when the guns begin to shoot.

113   In an only slightly exaggerated picture of the worldview of people who have made a mythical reality evaluation of a situation and the "logical" conclusions it leads to, James Branch Cabell writes:

"Was it not only yesterday" asks Jurgen of Satan, "one of the younger devils was brought before you, upon the charge that he had said the climate of Heaven was better than the climate here? . . . You should have remembered, Sir, that a devil whose patriotism has been impugned is a devil due to be punished: that there is no time to be prying into irrelevant questions of his guilt or innocence. Otherwise I take it, you will never have any real democracy in Hell."

Cabell, J. B., *Jurgen*, Robert McBride & Co., N.Y., 1919, p. 280.

As Ulysses S. Grant declared at the start of the Civil War, "There are now only two parties: patriots and traitors."

116   On February 26, 1991, the United States and other UN countries had been bombing Iraq very heavily for thirty-nine days. Although the literally thousands of air attacks each day were directed at "military" targets, there were a high number of Iraqi *civilian* casualties. (The term "military" included—in its subclass, "infrastructure"—power stations, communication centers, bridges, railroad stations, and other targets, which were frequently surrounded by civilian housing.) The U.S. had complete control of the air, could bomb at will, and no Iraqi planes were flying. During the night, an Iraqi Scud missile hit an American *army* barracks. About 30 *soldiers* were killed and many others wounded. The CBS news anchorman, Dan Rather, called this, "A deliberate and despicable act of terrorism."

116   Robert Kennedy speaking afterward of the Bay of Pigs disaster: "It seemed that, with John Kennedy leading us and with all that talent that he had developed, *nothing could stop us.*"

Quoted in Deikman, op. cit., p. 6.

Similar feelings were expressed by planners after the Gallipoli disaster in World War I and the Dieppe Raid fiasco in World War II. This is the illusion of invulnerability found in the mythic orientation: people believe that if their leader says an action will succeed, it will, even if it is very dangerous, rests on untested assumptions, and requires luck. Since this is a mythic view, the leader is not blamed afterward for the failure. Bad news and defeats in this orientation are seen as proof that progress is continuing and that we will eventually win.

117   James, op. cit.

117   The American public does not argue very much about taxes for defense. . . . But we hate paying taxes for education, low-cost housing, medical care for all, and other essentials of democratic society.

Rosenthal, A. M., *New York Times*, March 11, 1991, p. A27.

119   Gordon Allport quotes the anthropologist Clyde Kluckhorn as to the origin of the idea that every culture contains a varying amount of "free-floating aggression" which is periodically "drained off" in war.

Allport, G. W., *The Nature of Prejudice*, Addison-Wesley, Cambridge, Mass., 1954, p. 387.

The purpose of this concept of education is to keep the level of this "free-floating aggression" as low as possible by developing individuals who are secure and happy in their own being and in their group memberships. The "drain" is in projection and displacement, and the best way to prevent it pressing toward war is to lower it at its source—self-hatred, rejection of part of the self, and feelings of isolation and estrangement.

121 William James believed that peace as an enduring state was not possible unless the nations found a way to encompass in peace the virtues of the military—"intrepidity, teamwork, surrender of private interests" and so forth. The viewpoint of this book is that James is essentially correct, but that we must approach the problem on a deeper level. Surrender of private interests implies a shift of values to other realities in which other things are more important than the interests, or indeed the very life, of the individual. We must teach the individual to be at home in other realities than the sensory, in a way that binds us together with *all* other human life rather than one part of it against other parts.

Arnold Toynbee, in his *War and Civilization*, also writes of the "military virtues" and points out that their value lies in their virtue, not in their setting. He says that it flies in the face of all experience to believe that they can only be found in the horrible place in which they have been most frequently noted. He uses as an example the diamond, removed from the clay and set in a diadem.

123 Barnet, R., "After the Cold War," *The New Yorker*, January 1, 1990, p. 66.

124 While all other sciences have advanced, government is at a stand; little better practiced now than three or four thousand years ago.

U.S. president John Adams, quoted in Tuchman, op. cit., p. 4.

124 Tolstoy, L., op. cit., p. 564.

124 Tolstoy, op. cit., p. 1109.

125 Allport, G., "The Role of Expectancy," in Bramson and Goethals, op. cit. p. 178.

125 Dewey, J., *Problems of Men*, Philosophical Library, N.Y., 1946, p. 186.